THE LIFE OF THE PARTY

Celebrating Life with the Ultimate Joy-Giver

JASON J. NELSON

—WHAT PEOPLE ARE SAYING ABOUT THIS BOOK—

In *The Life of the Party*, Jason Nelson ushers us into Jesus' world with a vibrant retelling of Gospel narratives. We are present when Jesus cures the woman who has hemorrhaged for 12 years. We witness Jesus expelling professional mourners and bringing Jarius's young daughter back to life. Jason highlights how Jesus came to earth to bring life, hope, and salvation to everyone—men, women, and children. All we have to do is ask and follow Him.

—**Dr. Shelley Sekula-Gibbs, M.D.,** Former U.S. Congress Member
Former Houston City Council Member,
The Woodlands Township Board Director,
Wife, Grandmother, Catholic

Having never been the life of my own party, but being married to someone for over half a century who is, I found Jason's approach to these "parties" (social events) in the life of Jesus fascinating. Knowing Jason well as a part of our preaching and teaching team at Grace, and his outstanding communication and expository skills, I know each chapter will minister to you as you navigate the various life events we all walk through. Experiencing Jesus on His journey through life is a great way to discover how you should respond as you walk your own. I highly recommend *The Life of the Party*.

Steve Riggle, Pastor, Grace Woodlands Church

I have had the joy of knowing and serving alongside Pastor Jason Nelson as a friend, colleague, and fellow pastor, and I deeply respect his love for Jesus and for the people he shepherds. *The Life of the Party* reflects Jason's pastoral heart and his desire to help people encounter Christ in life-giving and transformative ways. With clarity, warmth, and faithfulness to Scripture, he invites readers to see Jesus as present, compassionate, and full of joy in the everyday moments of life. This book will encourage believers, strengthen faith, and gently draw seekers toward the hope and fullness found in Christ. I am grateful for this work and gladly commend it to the church.

—***Dr. Sam Thomas,*** Teaching Pastor, Grace Woodlands Church

Today's stressful world highlights the significant advantages of social interaction and support. We were created for community and to be around others. And who better to spend time with than Jesus? Jason masterfully uses the various social engagements throughout Jesus' ministry to craft a thought-provoking message. Readers can use each chapter to apply Jason's teachings to their lives in new and creative ways. Gain a fresh perspective as you learn how Jesus really is *the Life of the Party*!

—***Samuel Granberry,*** Retired UMC Pastor, Financial Advisor

Copyright © 2026 by Jason J. Nelson

All rights reserved. No part of this publication may be reproduced, distributed, or transmitted in any form or by any means, without prior written permission of the authors, except with brief quotations used in literary reviews and specific other non-commercial uses permitted by copyright law. For permission requests, please write to "Attention: Permissions Coordinator" at info@harvestcreek.net.

This book is a work of non-fiction. Every effort has been made to ensure that all the information on these pages was accurate at the time of publication.

The views expressed in this work are solely those of the author and do not necessarily reflect the views of the publisher.

Unless otherwise marked, scripture references are taken from the Holy Bible, New International Version®, NIV® Copyright ©1973, 1978, 1984, 2011 by Biblica, Inc.® Used by permission. All rights reserved worldwide.

Book Cover & Interior Layout © 2026 Harvest Creek Publishing & Design

Harvest Creek Publishing & Design
www.harvestcreek.net

The Life of the Party— 2nd ed.

ISBN 978-1-961641-45-7

Printed in The United States

—CONTENTS—

- —What People are Saying About This Book................2
- —Dedication................6
- —How to Use This Book................7
- —Foreword................9
- —Preface................12
- —Chapter 1 Beach Party................17
- —Chapter 2 Wedding Party................29
- —Chapter 3 Birthday Party................41
- —Chapter 4 Travel Party................53
- —Chapter 5 Pool Party................65
- —Chapter 6 Boat Party................77
- —Chapter 7 Royal Party................88
- —Chapter 8 House-Warming Party................98
- —Chapter 9 Dinner Party................108
- —Chapter 10 Surprise Party................119
- —Chapter 11 Dance Party................129
- —Chapter 12 The After Party!................139
- —About the Author................151

—DEDICATION—

To my wife, Tiffany: You are my inspiration.

To my mom and dad: Thank you for everything.

And to my children: I love you past the stars and back.

–HOW TO USE THIS BOOK–

THE LIFE OF THE PARTY was written to introduce people to the exciting, vibrant, compassionate, joy-filled life of Jesus as revealed in the Gospels. Whether you know nothing about Jesus, you're new to the Christian faith, or you're someone who's followed Jesus for years but longs for a fresh perspective, this book is for you.

Over the past five years, I've been humbled and encouraged to hear how this book has helped people discover the joy Jesus provides and has reinvigorated seasoned believers with a deeper appreciation for His life, light, and love.

In this updated edition, I've added two new chapters reinforcing the central theme of the book. I've also included questions at the end of each chapter, making this book a full study guide to help you go deeper—personally or with others. Here are a few simple ways to engage with this book:

- **Read it cover to cover.** Let the narrative unfold like a journey, walking with Jesus through stories that show His humanity, divinity, and the abundant life He offers.
- **Jump around.** If something in your life needs specific encouragement—healing, hope, forgiveness, or joy—feel free to flip to the chapters that speak directly to that need.
- **Use the book for a personal book study or within a Bible Study group.** This resource is designed to work well as a book study or

within a Bible study group, providing structure and discussion points that encourage growth and community.
- **Share the book as an evangelistic tool.** Books are a great way to introduce new people to Jesus in a relatable and accessible way, helping them discover who He is and what He offers.
- **Pray as you read.** Ask the Holy Spirit to help you see Jesus not only on the pages of Scripture but in your daily life. He still brings life and light wherever He goes.

My prayer is that as you read *The Life of the Party*, you'll come to know Jesus more personally and learn to walk with Him more joyfully.

—*Jason J. Nelson*

—FOREWORD—

WE ARE INTRODUCED to the word "party " early in life. Consider a child's first birthday party. Parents shower their little ones with balloons, streamers, and often an overwhelming number of gifts. Sometimes, these parties are as elaborate as weddings. I'm reminded of a recent clip about a new trend: parents throw huge birthday parties for their young kids who will not recall a thing. It makes one wonder if that kind of party isn't more for the parents than the child.

The word "party" has several meanings, the most prominent being a social gathering or celebration. A party brings people together for a special purpose, such as a birthday or a casual evening with friends. It can also refer to a group of soldiers or a group aligned with a particular viewpoint or opinion, as in a political party.

The concept of a party originated in the Anglo-French languages around the 14th century and stems from the root word "partir," which actually means to divide. Ironically, the origin of the word speaks to division. Yet, parties actually offer the chance for direct interaction and connection with people, something Jesus valued. In-person gatherings foster a sense of community and belonging. They are opportunities to build and honor traditions and to create a heritage.

Nowadays, people primarily use the internet to socialize and make friends. Yet, those experiences do not contain an atmosphere of food, music, laughter, and other expressions that involve the guests and encourage the social unity a party provides. Joy, fellowship, and celebration were part of God's original plan for humanity.

It might be tough to envision a book that features Jesus and parties together. For centuries, certain theologians have argued that Jesus was focused on one mission: to save humanity. Even some contemporary Christians struggle to comprehend the idea that the King of Kings ever took part in a festive event.

After all, He had sermons to prepare and healings and miracles to perform. Surely there was no time in His busy schedule for social gatherings and celebrations. Jesus was serious and solemn, not one to party. Right?

That is the source of a frequent misinterpretation. Jesus was definitely not a party-er. Most certainly not in the sense we think of today with coarse joking and wild, reckless behavior. No. The scripture is clear, as it warns against that type of empty lifestyle.

> Do not get drunk with wine,
> for that is debauchery, but be filled with the spirit.
> **EPHESIANS 5:18**

But Jesus did attend celebrations. And often. There are many recorded instances where Jesus was not only an honored guest but an active participant in these gatherings and feasts. In my opinion, those events were part of Jesus' best evangelistic work. It was a time when Jesus could show compassion and love. Celebrations were the setting for many of His miracles. They were the platform for Him to teach parables and convey spiritual truths.

The Son of God wasn't distant and unapproachable. Jesus brought joy and abundance to every gathering He attended. He wasn't opposed to parties; he embraced them as opportunities to bless others. Jesus interacted with everyone, offering mercy and compassion. There was a unique purpose in each gathering.

When Jesus attended a celebration, He brought people closer to the Father. Being the "light of the world," He ate with sinners, yet remained sin-free. The psalmist David wrote:

> This is the day that the Lord has made;
> let us rejoice and be glad in it.
> **PSALM 118:24**

I've interacted with Dr. Jason Nelson for many years, thanks to my ministry ties with the Grace International churches. He's a talented writer, making theology accessible and precise, yet in simple language. Within these pages, Jason outlines the many festivities, banquets, and events where Jesus engaged with others socially. These times weren't divisive or disagreeable. They were events where Jesus brought people together for a fresh experience of God's love. These were gatherings where he sparked serious, spiritual conversations and brought messages of hope to all attendees.

Be blessed as you reflect on the profound impact Jesus—the giver of joy—had on people through shared meals, celebrations, and meaningful moments. Discover the connection between salvation and celebration. Find renewed hope in the grace of Jesus, who was and is still *The Life of the Party*.

—*Dr. James L. Garlow,* Author, Communicator, Historian
Founder & CEO of Well Versed

—PREFACE—

SUNDAY, APRIL 18, 1982. This was the date I invited Jesus into my heart. Everything in my life changed after that significant date. On this day, my Savior forever saved my soul.

How do I remember it was this date? Because my dad has it written in his Bible. I was five years old. Yes, I know, I was very young. But even then, I was very aware of God's presence and His love.

Up to this special day, I had heard many stories about Jesus. As a young child in Sunday school, I learned all about who He is and what He promises to anyone who believes in Him. Jesus was in my mind but hadn't yet taken His rightful place on the throne of my heart.

Communion was being served at our country community church that morning. Just like every other Sunday morning before, my parents took Communion, but I didn't. This was not out of the ordinary, but this time, I felt left out. I really wanted to take Communion just like my parents did. On the way home from worship, I asked my dad why I couldn't take Communion and who was allowed to.

Dad looked at me through the rearview mirror and said, "Well, Jason, communion is for Christians; it's for anyone who trusts in Jesus and invites him into his or her life."

I said, "Well, I want to be a Christian."

Just recently, my dad and I reminisced about this story, recalling our conversation in the car. My father shared that my question about

Communion and becoming a Christian had caught him off guard because child evangelism had never crossed his mind. Even then, he recognized my seriousness and sincerity.

So that Sunday evening, at bedtime, my three-year-old brother, Ryan, and I went up to the bedroom we shared. Ryan hopped into his bed, and I jumped into mine. Dad came upstairs, as he always did, to tuck us in and to pray with us. But this night, this time, this prayer was different.

This time, I climbed out of my bed and knelt at my bedside. With my dad kneeling beside me, I prayed a simple prayer:

> *Jesus, I love you, and I know you love me. Forgive me of my sin. Come into my life. Be my Savior and my Lord. Amen.*

That night, according to Paul's words, as recorded in Ephesians, I was "sealed by the Holy Spirit."

And you also were included in Christ when you heard the message of truth, the gospel of your salvation. When you believed, you were marked in him with a seal, the promised Holy Spirit.
EPHESIANS 1:13

Immediately afterward, I looked at my dad and said, "What about Ryan?"

My dad recently informed me that I had started showing an evangelistic mindset and concern for Ryan from that moment on. That's ironic since I beat up on him all the time, as big brothers do.

On that quiet night in 1982, after I asked about Ryan, Dad said, "Well, Jason, Jesus loves Ryan, too. But he's still a little young to understand what it means to ask Jesus into his heart. But when he gets a little older, he can pray the same prayer you prayed."

From that day on, I took Communion as often as I could, and every time afterward, I would ask my dad, "What about Ryan?"

Fast-forward a few years. I was eight, and Ryan was six. It was Communion Sunday again. During Sunday school earlier that day, Ryan's teacher taught about Holy Communion, explaining what it is and who participates in it.

After church, Ryan's teacher cornered my dad and said, "Jon, I need to talk to you about Ryan."

According to Dad, his initial thought was, *What? Ryan? This can't be right. Ryan never gets in trouble. Trouble doesn't follow Ryan; it follows Jason, but not Ryan.*

She went on to inform my father that Ryan had mentioned he couldn't receive Communion. When asked why, Ryan replied, "My dad won't let me be a Christian."

It goes without saying that my dad began laughing and gave the teacher a clear explanation of the situation. We followed our usual routine that night; Ryan and I both hopped into bed. Dad came into our room to pray with us.

However, before he prayed, he had a conversation with Ryan regarding what Ryan had mentioned in Sunday school earlier that morning. Dad explained to Ryan how to become a Christian and what it meant to live like one.

Dad said, "Ryan, when you confess your sin and invite Jesus into your life, that means Jesus lives inside of you, and he helps you become a better boy."

Well, Ryan didn't say anything for a few moments. And then, with a puzzled expression on his face, he looked at Dad, then at me, then at Dad again, and said, "Well, how come He isn't helping Jason?"

I got mad and said, "Yes, He is!" Then I threw my pillow at Ryan—in brotherly love, of course.

Every time I reflect on these two experiences, which many would refer to as conversion stories, my eyes are opened even more to an amazing truth: Jesus loves me, and Jesus loves you.

I hope you come to realize this powerful reality more and more every day. By reading this book, I also hope you will grow in your relationship with Jesus, *the Life of the Party*, and receive everything He offers you.

One day, as Jesus was standing by the Lake of Gennesaret, the people were crowding around him and listening to the word of God. He saw at the water's edge two boats, left there by the fishermen, who were washing their nets. He got into one of the boats, the one belonging to Simon, and asked him to put out a little from shore. Then he sat down and taught the people from the boat. When he had finished speaking, he said to Simon, "Put out into deep water, and let down the nets for a catch."

Simon answered, "Master, we've worked hard all night and haven't caught anything. But because you say so, I will let down the nets."

When they had done so, they caught such a large number of fish that their nets began to break. So they signaled their partners in the other boat to come and help them, and they came and filled both boats so full that they began to sink. When Simon Peter saw this, he fell at Jesus' knees and said, "Go away from me, Lord; I am a sinful man!" For he and all his companions were astonished at the catch of fish they had taken, and so were James and John, the sons of Zebedee, Simon's partners.

Then Jesus said to Simon, "Don't be afraid; from now on you will fish for people." So they pulled their boats up on shore, left everything, and followed him.

LUKE 5: 1-11

—CHAPTER 1—
Beach Party

NOBODY LIKES a deadbeat. That's a fair statement, isn't it? Hanging around lazy and lackluster people is draining. And I've never heard of someone referred to as the *"death* of the party." Am I right? Even if such a person did exist and we happened to be at the same party, I'd keep my distance.

Yeah, I know. That's not very WWJD [What would Jesus do?] of me. But I'm just being real with you. Besides, I'm more a proponent of WWPD [What would Peter do?] because Peter sets the bar ridiculously low in the Gospels—just high enough for me to reach it—most days.

Anyway, when you think about it, the truth is that we aren't drawn to death. We gravitate toward life. We're naturally attracted to people who are lively, dynamic, and charismatic. Like a paper clip to a magnet, we gravitate toward people who have a unique and special energy to them—people who have that Je ne sais quoi. These individuals are bubbly, optimistic, upbeat, and so happy.

Not only are we drawn to these individuals, but after encounters with positive people, we often walk away with a pep in our step. We have a deep yearning to know them better or maybe even a desire to become more like them.

BEING DRAWN TO JESUS

Jesus is one of these people. In fact, no one in history has ever matched the level of Jesus' liveliness, energy, and charisma. The power of His presence is off the charts. Jesus was the original *Life of the Party*.

And He remains the *Life of the Party* today. Of course, this makes sense, right? After all, Jesus is "the way and the truth and the life."

> Jesus answered, "I am the way and the truth and the life. No one comes to the Father except through me."
> JOHN 14:6

As far as I know, Jesus is the only person ever to say, "I have come that they may have life, and have it to the full."

> The thief comes only to steal and kill and destroy; I have come that they may have life, and have it to the full.
> JOHN 10:10

Only Jesus has ever extended this abundant life to others, free of charge.

An Anglican priest named John Wesley seemed to understand this. This eighteenth-century preacher's kid and preacher came to embrace the full and magnetic life Jesus has and offers to all those who believe in him. Wesley spent his whole life passionately talking about the life Jesus gives.

Even though he was rejected a lot, Wesley never stopped believing in the Bible's ability to unleash the power of heaven. Despite much ridicule, John Wesley never stopped believing in the power of the Holy Spirit to use God's Word to transform a person's heart. Though he was kicked to the curb—sometimes literally—Wesley never stopped enthusiastically telling people about Jesus.

Because he was passionately persistent, fiercely determined, and unabashedly faithful to the message of Christ, Wesley's efforts paid off in a big way. He traveled more than 250,000 miles on horseback to preach. And get this: he preached more than 40,000 sermons to thousands of people without any advanced amplification system. There were no microphones or megaphones. My throat hurts just thinking about having to talk that much or that loudly to that many people.

John Wesley is proof that if you're excited about living for Jesus, people will take notice. He's proof that if you're passionate about sharing the love and message of Christ, you'll inspire others. He really is proof positive, in the words of an adage, that if you "catch on fire with enthusiasm, people will come from miles to watch you burn."

John Wesley enthusiastically proclaimed the good news of Jesus Christ, and people responded by the thousands. Can you imagine? That's a lot of *Just as I Am* choruses!

Drawing a crowd was a talent that John Wesley developed. And where did he learn this? How did Wesley discover how to be so magnetic? Who taught him how to attract a large audience? Jesus did! *Please tell me you saw that coming.*

John Wesley opened his Bible, read about Jesus' work, and then followed Jesus' example. Long before Wesley was born, thousands of people came to see and hear from Jesus because He burned with love for people. And because Jesus enthusiastically lived and preached an inspirational message full of life.

Read the Gospels, and you'll quickly see that Jesus draws a crowd everywhere He goes. Wherever Jesus is, He becomes the *Life of the Party*. And not just because He does something that makes Him the center of attention, although raising actual deadbeats from the grave will undoubtedly get you noticed.

THE LIFE-GIVING TRAITS OF JESUS

Jesus also becomes *the Life of the Party* because He brings and gives life wherever He is. In Luke's story, people have come from all over the area, from miles away, to hear Jesus speak. On this day, another sizeable crowd is forming all around Jesus.

Can you picture the scene? Give it a try. Close your eyes and imagine being there—just for a few moments, though, because you've got some more reading to do. In your mind's eye, visualize this story.

Here's Jesus standing on the shore beside the Sea of Galilee, also known as the Lake of Gennesaret. Sand is clinging to His legs and sticking to the hair on His arms. The sand between His toes is gently being rinsed away each time a wave washes in and reaches the top of His ankles.

A cool, steady breeze coming off the water is blowing through His hair, bringing with it a faint but familiar scent of freshly caught fish. Seagulls fly overhead as Jesus continues to describe the kingdom of God, His words matching the rhythm of the rolling tide behind him.

Got it now? Are you there?

Behind Jesus is the Sea of Galilee, a beautiful body of water. In front of Him is a sea of humanity staring back at Him, hanging on every word He says. As Jesus teaches, the crowd continues to grow. There are people everywhere. They're gathering all over the hillside. They're lounging on the sand. They're sitting on top of rocks and stumps. Some of the older kids are wading in the water. There are countless people along the shoreline, and more are arriving.

The crowd grows larger and larger by the minute. Jesus seems to know that everyone in the crowd on this day needs to hear what He has to say, so He becomes resourceful in a way only He can. He seems to know He's got to find a way to make it possible for the people in the back of the crowd and on the periphery to hear Him better.

Jesus looks around for a moment or two and locates a boat. He calls a time-out, walks over to the boat, and finds some fishermen there. And what are they doing? Washing their nets.

Now, isn't this an interesting contrast? Hundreds, maybe thousands, of people have flocked to Jesus to hear Him speak, but these fishermen have not. These guys aren't there to hear Jesus speak. They're not standing along the shoreline to catch a sermon. These men are there to finish their work so they can go home.

They've been fishing all night long—because that's the best time to fish the Sea of Galilee—and have caught nothing. They're beat. Tired. Exhausted. So, they aren't going to take the time or energy to listen to Jesus.

And get this: Jesus is talking about life-altering, life-changing, life-transforming, eternally significant matters. But all that matters to these guys is cleaning up their fishing gear. Jesus is delivering the most powerful message of hope and love the world has ever heard, but these guys aren't listening. Instead, they're wallowing in self-pity—something we never do, of course—because they have worked hard all night long for nothing.

Here, Jesus is captivating the crowd with talk of things like washing away their sins. But these fishermen aren't paying any attention to Jesus at all. Why? Because they're too *busy, busy, busy* washing their nets.

These guys are so tired, so distracted, and so stressed out. They don't have fish to trade on this particular day. No fish equals no income.

Yet Jesus walks over to these tired, distracted, and stressed-out fishermen and asks Simon, who later becomes Peter, to take Him on a boat ride just a little way from shore so everyone in the crowd can see and hear Him better. Surprisingly, Peter agrees. He obeys.

Even though he's probably not in the mood to get back on the water, he does what Jesus asks him to do. He throws his half-washed fishing net back in his boat and takes Jesus out just a little way from the shore.

Time-out. Do you see what Jesus is doing?

This is ingenious. It's brilliant, which shouldn't really be that surprising since this is Jesus we're talking about.

Jesus is taking advantage of the unique geography surrounding the Sea of Galilee. He has put himself in a position where He can use the water as a natural amplifier. Because the terrain of this shoreline is filled with inlets, Jesus is positioning Himself on the boat in front of the crowd in a way that creates a natural amphitheater.

Jesus is making it possible for everyone on land to see and hear Him, and at the same time, He's forcing Peter to listen. Peter becomes a captive listener because he's out on the boat with Jesus, listening to Jesus preach.

Now the crowd is being saturated by the Word of God *on land.* And Simon Peter is being saturated by the Word of God *on the water.* Peter's mind and heart are being bombarded with truth. Jesus' message of love, hope, and forgiveness is winning Peter over. It's convincing him to put his faith in Jesus and to trust in this teacher he hardly knows.

After Jesus finishes teaching, he looks at Peter and tells him it's time to go fishing—a second time.

Time-out. Again.

Have you ever felt God asking you to do something that doesn't make sense and seems ridiculous? Well, this doesn't make sense to Peter. What Jesus is asking Peter to do seems ridiculous on the surface. You can't catch fish when the sun is high and bright. If you actually want to catch fish, you don't fish the Sea of Galilee during the day in deep waters; you fish at night in shallow waters.

Peter could easily have responded by saying something like, "Listen, Jesus, I know we don't know each other very well. You seem like a nice guy who wants to help everyone. But you obviously don't know what you're talking about. You can't fish now and expect to catch anything. It doesn't make sense."

Or Peter could have responded with something like, "What makes you qualified to tell me how to fish, huh, Jesus? What? Do you think you know more about fishing than I do? I've been fishing for years. My dad was a fisherman, his dad was a fisherman, and his dad's dad was a fisherman. So why don't I just drop you back off on the shore so you can do what you do and leave the fishing to me?"

Peter could have said something like that, but he didn't. His response isn't hostile. It's gentle, honest, and vulnerable. Peter looks at Jesus and says, "Master, we have worked all night long and haven't caught anything."

Peter's response reflects a weary and worn man. But it also reflects a man who is willing to trust and obey. Even if, and even when, the request seems unreasonable. And in the same breath, Peter says, "But because you say so, I will let down the nets."

THE MIRACLE AWAITS US

What happens next is amazing. Because Peter obeys Jesus, he experiences a miracle. Peter catches more fish than he can even handle. The impossible has just happened. This is a big deal for a fisherman, but it's an even bigger deal for a sinner.

Suddenly, Peter's eyes are opened to the reality of who Jesus is. Jesus is more than just a popular preacher, more than a wandering prophet, and more than an insightful teacher. Peter catches a glimpse of Jesus' power and holiness.

Peter is driven to his knees. He yells out, "Go away from me, Lord, for I am a sinful man."

Peter is immediately humbled in the same way the Prophet Isaiah is humbled in the Old Testament when he says:

"Woe to me... I am ruined! For I am a man of unclean lips, and I live among a people of unclean lips, (cont'd next page)

> and my eyes have seen the King, the Lord Almighty."
> ISAIAH 6:5

Like Isaiah, Peter is completely in awe of the Lord. And he is also afraid. He's never seen power like this, and he's terrified. And as he's shaking with fear, Jesus looks at Peter and says, "Don't be afraid; from now on you will catch people."

Peter immediately leaves everything behind, including his boat, his fish, his potential profits, and his fishing gear. He drops his net and follows Jesus.

In this story, on this day, we don't know how many lives were changed by Jesus. But we do know at least one life was changed: Peter's. Peter's life was radically changed.

And that's the main miracle in this story. The main miracle isn't the miracle in the water; it's the miracle on the boat. It isn't Peter's miraculous catch of fish, as amazing as that is. The main miracle is Peter's transformation from a fisher of *fish* to a fisher of *people*.

Jesus takes a simple fisherman and assigns his purpose in life, all in one day's work. Peter drops his net and follows Jesus. Then, Jesus employs and empowers Peter to transform the world.

After Peter receives the Holy Spirit, he becomes contagiously enthusiastic about the gospel. Peter catches on fire for Jesus, and people come from miles away to watch him burn. Jesus used Peter to turn the world upside down. And to think it all started because Peter chose to drop his net and follow Jesus.

Now, this is where you and I come into the story—if we choose to do so. See, if we want to follow Jesus, we have to be willing to drop our nets. Jesus says it this way in Luke:

> "Whoever wants to be my disciple must deny themselves
> and take up their cross daily and follow me."
> LUKE 9:23B

Did you catch what Jesus said in this passage? Jesus said, "daily." Dropping our nets, denying ourselves, and following Jesus is a daily endeavor that requires a daily commitment.

But what does that look like? Well, in light of this story, following Jesus means waking up each day saying, "Jesus, today I will get in the boat with You. I want to go where You go and be where You are. Wherever I am, at work or at play, I will do my best to remind myself that You are always with me."

Following Jesus also means making sure we don't become so busy, busy, busy—so consumed with "washing our nets"—that we miss out on taking time throughout our day to fill our hearts and minds with God's Word.

We have God's Truth at our fingertips.

Hello? Please read that again.

The words Jesus spoke on the shore of the Sea of Galilee are in your Bible. No matter where we are on our faith journey, we must immerse ourselves in the Bible and let the Bible transform us. Following Jesus means complete obedience, as Peter shows us in this story.

There will be times when we feel God is leading us to do something that doesn't make sense, at least *to us*. In those moments, our response shouldn't be, "Well, God, you don't know what you're talking about. I'm not qualified to apply for that job. I'm not gifted enough to teach that Bible Study. I'm not smart enough to get into that school. I don't have the time to volunteer for that ministry."

Nope. Just like most excuses, those are pretty poor. When Jesus tells us to do something—no matter what it is—our response should be the same as Peter's. "But because you say so, I will."

Following Jesus means living with an attitude of humility and having a deep reverence for God and the holiness of God. Just like Peter shows us. Considering God's holiness, following Jesus means seeking forgiveness for our sins and praying for the Holy Spirit to make us more like Jesus.

There are three crucial considerations to keep in mind when following Jesus. We must seriously heed our responsibility to:

1. Fish for people.
2. Share the love and message of Jesus with others.
3. Take care of people who are hurting or feeling helpless.

Finally, following Jesus means dropping nets and surrendering our lives to Him every day. It's about laying all our hopes, dreams, desires, ambitions, and plans down at His feet. And living the God-given dreams God has for each one of us.

In a boat on the Sea of Galilee, Peter encountered Jesus, the living Son of God. The result? He was never the same again. Every day, through the power of the Holy Spirit, we can drop our nets and come into contact with this same Jesus.

The more we hang around Jesus, the more the fullness of His life flows in and through us. And it's this Jesus-giving life that will ignite us on fire with enthusiasm, so people will come from miles away to watch *us* burn.

 **THOUGHT-PROVOKING PARTY FOOD**

1. The French phrase **Je ne sais quoi** literally translates to "I don't know what." It refers to an inexplicable quality or trait that attracts people to an individual. It conveys someone who possesses an enigmatic allure that fascinates. Can you think of someone in your life's journey who has captivated your attention? What was it that attracted you to them?

2. Why was Jesus' life and His ministry on earth so captivating to those who encountered him?

3. Describe Peter's response to Jesus. How was it different from that of the other fishermen? Have you ever chosen to go a specific direction as guided by the Holy Spirit, even if it meant leaving the crowd?

4. Before Jesus does the miraculous in our lives, He often asks us to do something that might seem impossible to us. What is Jesus calling you to do in light of this passage?

5. Jesus gives Peter a new role: to fish for people. This is also a responsibility He gives to all of us in the Great Commission, where He instructs us to "go and make disciples." What opportunities is He giving you today to make disciples...to fish for people?

On the third day, a wedding took place at Cana in Galilee. Jesus' mother was there, and Jesus and his disciples had also been invited to the wedding. When the wine was gone, Jesus' mother said to him, "They have no more wine."

"Woman, why do you involve me?" Jesus replied. "My hour has not yet come."

His mother said to the servants, "Do whatever he tells you."

Nearby stood six stone water jars, the kind used by the Jews for ceremonial washing, each holding from twenty to thirty gallons. Jesus said to the servants, "Fill the jars with water"; so they filled them to the brim. Then he told them, "Now draw some out and take it to the master of the banquet."

They did so, and the master of the banquet tasted the water that had been turned into wine. He did not realize where it had come from, though the servants who had drawn the water knew. Then he called the bridegroom aside and said, "Everyone brings out the choice wine first and then the cheaper wine after the guests have had too much to drink; but you have saved the best till now."

What Jesus did here in Cana of Galilee was the first of the signs through which he revealed his glory, and his disciples believed in him. After this he went down to Capernaum with His mother and brothers and His disciples. There they stayed for a few days.

JOHN 2:1-12

—CHAPTER 2—
Wedding Party

IT DOESN'T REALLY MATTER where my family and I go to eat, because 99% of the time, my son, Brooks, is going to order chicken fingers and French fries. When the kids were much younger, we decided to have lunch at Olive Garden one Sunday after church services. Like most Sundays, we all walked in nearly famished, probably because the preacher got a little long-winded (you can probably imagine who was preaching that day).

We couldn't get the breadsticks to our table fast enough, and when they finally arrived, they were gone in about thirty seconds. When our waiter returned with two more baskets, we placed our order. Everyone chose some sort of Italian dish—except for Brooks. He ordered... chicken fingers and French fries. Shocker, right?

The food arrived about ten minutes later, and everyone started diving in. Hannah, my oldest, was enjoying her Italian cuisine when she looked over at her brother and said, "Brooks, can I have one of your French fries?"

He looked at her and said, "Nope."

She tried again: "Come on, Brooks, can I just have one French fry?"

Again, while stuffing his face, he said, "No."

That's when I stepped in. I saw this as a timely parenting moment, so I said, "Brooks, come on, man—give your sister a French fry." Then I added, "What would Jesus do?"

He looked at me, without missing a beat, and said, "He'd make more French fries."

Of course, He would. What was I thinking? Perhaps I needed a little more childlike faith. This is Jesus, the One who can do the seemingly impossible. The one who walked on water and calmed the storm, healed the sick and raised the dead, cast out demons, and fed the five thousand.

And he's the one who made more... wine at a wedding in Cana of Galilee.

Yep. We're going to join Jesus in Cana of Galilee and watch Him do the miraculous.

As you can probably already tell by now, Jesus is a fairly popular guy. He spends a lot of time around a lot of people, and He seems to enjoy it. He loves to mingle with the masses, work the crowds, shake a few hands, and kiss a few babies.

He loves people, and people love Him.

He's popular.

And for many reasons. Jesus is full of life, of course. He's the source of life, so that makes sense.

He's also full of energy, passion, and enthusiasm. He's charismatic, so people are drawn to him.

Wherever Jesus goes, He becomes *the Life of the Party!* He immediately becomes the center of attention, and not just because He's performing miracles. Even before all the healings, people ran to Jesus because He loves people and brings them joy.

The more people get to know Jesus, the more they experience the joy He brings and the love He offers, and the more popular He becomes.

And the more popular He becomes, the more time people want to spend with Him.

Some people, like the disciples mentioned in the passage we'll explore today, want to spend the rest of their lives with Jesus. Even if it means walking in His dust and living in His shadow day after day after day, which is a great place for a disciple to be, by the way.

Then there are others who simply want to meet the Man and sit down and eat with Him. So, much like Zacchaeus, they invite Jesus into their homes for a home-cooked meal and a chance to liven up their lives with the light of His presence.

And there are countless other people who, when they find out Jesus is in town, drop whatever they are doing in the moment just for the opportunity to see Him, even from a distance, and hear Him speak.

Finally, there are those who want Jesus to be a part of their most intimate and meaningful moments in life, so they invite Him to important life celebrations, such as weddings. And this is where we find Jesus in John 2:1-12.

Jesus—*the Life of the Party*—is at a wedding.

Jesus attends weddings, and just like any other wedding guest, is there to celebrate. He's there to have a good time. He's there to have fun! Yes, Jesus enjoys having fun too!

In the ancient context, weddings were big celebrations, even more so than our modern-day weddings. Life was tough back then, so the people lived for joyful festivities like these. Believe it or not, ancient weddings were huge productions, huge celebrations!

THE SIGNIFICANCE OF THE WINE

Weddings were highlights in life, mountaintop experiences for the entire community. They were one of life's greatest joys, and that's why it becomes such a big deal when the wine runs out!

In ancient Jewish thought, wine was essential to life, but not because it made people feel good, set the mood, lightened people up, or created a collective buzz.

No, in ancient daily life, wine was important because it was a vital source of drink. It was a healthier alternative to the contaminated water found in many of the town's wells. It's no wonder that it was an essential feature at every ancient Jewish wedding!

Wine wasn't offered so that people could get drunk and go wild. That was considered disgraceful and highly unlikely since the wine they drank back then was composed of two parts wine to three parts water. Wine was an essential feature at ancient Jewish weddings because it symbolized joy.

Throughout the ages, Jewish theologians have said, "Without wine, there is no joy!" Wine equals joy in the ancient context.

So what happened if you ran out of wine, especially on the first night of a celebration? Forget about it. The party's over. Go home, because whatever joy was present in the midst of this celebration just left the room.

And that's exactly what is about to happen at this wedding in Cana, as the passage tells us.

The celebration has just started, and the wine has already run out, so joy is actually on its way out the front door. The party has barely begun, but one of the guests has just lapped up the last drop of this pure, sweet, liquid joy.

The wine runs out. And if nobody does anything about it, the joy will run out as well!

Now we don't know why the wine runs out. I mean, we can speculate. Maybe the host didn't buy enough. Maybe Jesus' disciples ended up drinking more than their share. I can see Peter doing that. He seems like the type of guy who's always hanging around the punch bowl.

Or maybe it was a hot night, and people were just *really* thirsty.

Maybe there were some wedding crashers. There always are, aren't there? Perhaps a young kid came by and knocked over the tray of drinks.

We don't know.

We don't know why the wine runs out. But whatever the reason, this is extremely embarrassing for the host. You don't run out of wine. It is in bad form. It is horrible hospitality.

If the guests find out that the wine is all gone, not only will the host be embarrassed, but he'll also be ridiculed.

And the bride and groom will be humiliated.

The joy of the occasion will be stripped away because the symbol for joy—the wine—is gone!

Mary is the first to notice the wine is gone. And who does she turn to? Jesus. She tells him that the wine is gone, and what does he say?

Jesus looks at his mother and says, "My time has not yet come."

Well, Mary doesn't like his answer. And even though Jesus hasn't done anything miraculous in His life up to this moment, His mother knows who Jesus is and knows that if there's anyone who can fix this problem, it's Jesus.

Mary has faith in her son; she remembers that the angel told her years ago that He is the Son of God!

So, in this case, *Mama knows best.*

When Jesus says, "My time has not yet come," Mary seems to think, *Oh, yes, it has!*

She quickly spots the servants at the party, runs over to them, and says, "Hey, see that guy sitting over there so nonchalantly on that marble slab, so calm and cool, acting like his time hasn't come? Go over to him and do whatever he tells you to do!"

So they go over to Him.

Now, I'm pretty sure Jesus saw this coming. And whatever doubt He might have had about this being His time to shine must have gone away because He immediately evaluates His surroundings and locates six empty, twenty-to-thirty-gallon, stone-cold jars.

These stone jars were typically used to store water, allowing people to wash their hands and feet with ease.

These jars were never used to hold clean water.

You'd never think of drinking the water from these pots, as it's reserved for rinsing only. Jesus looks over at these jars, points to them, and then tells the servants to fill them to the brim with water.

What? Well, that doesn't make sense!

If I were a servant and Jesus told me to fill these jars with water, I would have thought, *Come on, Jesus! Why do we need more water in these jars? People have already cleaned up. They've already rinsed their hands and feet. They're already eating. Can't this wait till tomorrow?*

Besides, Jesus, people don't drink from these jars. And anyway, we don't need more water, Jesus. We need more wine!

We don't know what the servants were thinking, but we do know that they heard Jesus and obeyed. And because they obey, because they hear Jesus' words and follow His command, because they don't argue with Jesus but willingly follow His instructions, a miracle happens.

Water becomes wine!

And not just any wine, but the finest wine one could offer or drink. The very best wine around. The "choice wine."

In a moment, the power of Christ is unleashed on a small part of the creation that He created as God, along with God the Father and the Holy Spirit.

When the power of God in Christ comes upon the water in these jars—in a manner that defies human comprehension—despair turns into hope, embarrassment and humiliation turn into pride, and emptiness turns into fullness.

- The undrinkable becomes drinkable.
- The insignificant becomes significant.
- The ordinary becomes extraordinary.

- The irrelevant becomes relevant.
- The tasteless becomes succulent.
- The bland becomes sweet.
- The impure becomes pure.
- The meaningless becomes meaningful, and
- The invaluable becomes valuable.

These common, ordinary, insignificant jars—these barren and now useless vessels waiting in the shadows—become, in a moment, extraordinary containers of pure joy!

Good wine is created, enabling the celebration to continue. Joy is created and restored, and it's all because of Jesus! Jesus creates and restores joy!

And not only does He create and restore joy, but He does so with abundance.

Jesus' miracle makes it possible for this celebration to continue for days. He creates 180 gallons of wine, the symbol of joy.

Jesus is the reason why the fun continues.

The guests might not know what Jesus has done, or the wedding party, or the wedding parents, but His mother knows, the servants know, and Jesus' disciples know!

They know who *the Life of the Party* is! They know where—or better yet, from whom—joy comes. They know joy comes from Jesus.

Jesus is in the business of distributing joy! He creates joy and then generously and abundantly gives it away. He pours joy out heavily and graciously upon humanity and upon His church.

Not only is Jesus in the joy-making and distributing business, but He's also the embodiment and personification of joy.

Who is Jesus?

He's not just *the Life of the Party* wherever He is, whether that's at a wedding celebration in Cana or in a room full of worshipers. Jesus is also the source of all joy. That's who Jesus is.

DISCOVERING WHO WE ARE

But who are we? Who are we in this story? Well, at times, we are the empty, stone-cold jars that have been used and set aside by the world.

We are the barren vessels sitting in the shadows who are, through the power of the Holy Spirit, being filled up to the brim with the joy of Christ.

Who are we?

We are members of the wedding party—totally unaware, at times, of what Jesus is doing behind the scenes of life to maximize the divine joy in us, around us, and through us.

Who are we?

We are the servants in this passage who are given the task of filling up the jars with water. Jesus is asking us to exercise our faith and help Him distribute His joy.

Who are we?

Each of us is the servant who brought the cup of wine to the master of the banquet. We are the ones who Jesus commands to bring His joy to those people who have never tasted anything so good and so pure.

Who are we?

We are the guests at the celebration. We are the ones who get to celebrate joy, not just for a day or two, but for a lifetime.

As followers of Jesus, we have the opportunity to experience the joy of Jesus as often as we desire.

We can tap into His ever-flowing joy, every single day!

But unfortunately, the distractions of this life often stand between us and the joy of the Lord.

The business and busyness of life have a way of draining us of our joy and distracting us from doing what we can do to tap into the joy Jesus offers. And when we're drained and distracted, we end up walking around this world with a hollowness in our hearts and a void within our souls.

But here's the good news again: Jesus loves us. Jesus cares about us. Jesus offers us abundant life.

Jesus is readily willing and lovingly longing to flood these empty vessels with his joy—*if* we let him.

See here's the thing: if we want to know the joy of the Lord, then we've got to go *to* the Lord of joy. The Psalms say it this way:

You have made known to me the path of life;
You will fill me with joy in Your presence.
PSALM 16:11

Every day, we can drink in the joy of the Lord. Every day, we can connect with Jesus and taste the joy He gives. Every single day, we can receive the joy that comes from spending one-on-one time with the Maker and Giver of joy.

All we have to do is open our Bibles and join Him in Cana.

And there's really no better time of the day to take in the joy of the Lord than in the morning.

Weeping may stay for the night. But joy comes in the morning.
PSALM 30:5

The joy we get from Jesus, early in the morning, will be the fuel we need to push through the obstacles, hardships, or adversity of our day.

Many of us wouldn't even think about leaving the house without first drinking a cup of coffee.

Yet there are days when we walk out the doors of our homes into a harsh, hostile, hollow, and pessimistic world without *first* drinking from the cup of joy that Jesus offers.

Remember, if we want to experience the joy of the Lord, we must *go to* the Lord of joy.

And the more we go to the Lord of joy, the more we live into the Truth, the biblical Truth that we find in the Old Testament.

Nehemiah 8:10 says, *The joy of the Lord is our strength.*

So it doesn't matter how we woke up today—feeling bad, feeling fine, or somewhere in between. What matters is how we live today.

What matters is that we choose Jesus. Choosing Jesus is choosing joy and His power, which comes with it.

What matters is that we take time each day to chat with the Creator, Sustainer, and Giver of joy.

What matters is that we wake up each morning and take a big gulp of his joy, maybe even while sipping coffee.

What matters is that after we have received the joy of the Lord, we praise the Lord of joy for who He is and what He has done.

And whenever Jesus miraculously turns your sorrow into joy, what matters is that you remember this truth: Jesus can do the impossible...He can make more French fries.

 **THOUGHT-PROVOKING PARTY FOOD**

1. Why do you think Jesus chose a wedding reception to perform His first miracle?

2. Once again, Jesus asks ordinary people (servants) to do something that seems illogical. Why do you think He does that?

3. In this chapter, it was mentioned that through the power of God in Christ, "Ordinary becomes extraordinary." How is that relevant to us?

4. Where do you see yourself in this story?

5. What is the "joy of the Lord," and how can it become your strength?

Now there was a Pharisee, a man named Nicodemus, who was a member of the Jewish ruling council. He came to Jesus at night and said, "Rabbi, we know that you are a teacher who has come from God. For no one could perform the signs you are doing if God were not with him."

Jesus replied, "Very truly I tell you, no one can see the kingdom of God unless they are born again."

"How can someone be born when they are old?" Nicodemus asked. "Surely they cannot enter a second time into their mother's womb to be born!"

Jesus answered, "Very truly I tell you, no one can enter the kingdom of God unless they are born of water and the Spirit. Flesh gives birth to flesh, but the Spirit gives birth to spirit. You should not be surprised at my saying, 'You must be born again.' The wind blows wherever it pleases. You hear its sound, but you cannot tell where it comes from or where it is going. So it is with everyone born of the Spirit."

"How can this be?" Nicodemus asked.

"You are Israel's teacher," said Jesus, "and do you not understand these things? Very truly I tell you, we speak of what we know, and we testify to what we have seen, but still you people do not accept our testimony. I have spoken to you of earthly things and you do not believe; how then will you believe if I speak of heavenly things? No one has ever gone into heaven except the one who came from heaven—the Son of Man. Just as Moses lifted up the snake in the wilderness, so the Son of Man must be lifted up, that everyone who believes may have eternal life in him."

For God so loved the world that he gave his one and only Son, that whoever believes in him shall not perish but have eternal life. For God did not send his Son into the world to condemn the world, but to save the world through him.

JOHN 3:1-17

–CHAPTER 3–
Birthday Party

THIS STORY INVOLVES one of the most profound and in-depth discussions of all time. In this conversation, Jesus introduces a brand-new concept into the history of human thought—a concept that will astound Nicodemus.

Immediately before our story and their conversation, though, Jesus arrives in Jerusalem as *the Life of the Party* once again.

At this point, his popularity is at its highest. As soon as Jesus enters the city, people swarm Him, which isn't surprising, right? We've seen over the last two chapters how the Man is like a magnet.

When Jesus enters Jerusalem, people rush to meet Him. No shocker. I mean, wouldn't you?

They want to hug Him, ask Him questions, or hear what He has to say about life, love, and the kingdom of God.

Or they run to Jesus because they want to be healed.

Of course, Jesus ministers to the people because He loves them.

But after He pours life and love into their lives, Jesus goes up into the temple. He is shocked at what He finds. People are selling and buying cattle, sheep, and goats. The temple, which is supposed to be a place of worship, has basically become a flea market. Jesus sees this and is furious.

Wait. Can Jesus get angry? Yes, He can, and yes, He does. But His anger is holy. It's justified.

Jesus creates quite a scene in the temple. Do you remember the story?

Try to visualize the scene for this experience as well. As soon as Jesus sees the temple being violated, He literally begins tossing tables.

And He's doing this in the middle of the crowd. Jesus, *the Life of the Party*, is creating chaos that will actually make it impossible for anyone, after this, to have an opportunity to meet with Him one-on-one.

This is why Nicodemus will have to meet Jesus at night. After this temple incident, you can't get Jesus alone. He's even more popular.

The crowds begin thinking, *Hey, this guy has no fear. He can't be stopped. No one can stand in His way. He's got to be the Messiah, the new King of Israel.* Which means life around Jesus is going to get even crazier.

Hey, I understand crazy. Maybe you do too?

THE NEEDS OF THE HUMAN CONDITION

When the kids were all at home, my family and I were living the wild and chaotic life. There was never a dull moment in our lives.

A few years back, on a Monday morning, everybody woke up ten minutes later than usual, which apparently makes a big difference in the Nelson home. We were all busting it to get ready for school and work.

I immediately started making breakfast because on most mornings, I assume the role of Chef Boyar-Jay. Here I was, scrambling eggs and flipping pancakes, thinking, *I've got this.*

While I was trying to find the butter, my son, Brooks, decided he was going to get chocolate milk for everyone. While pouring chocolate milk into his cup, he knocked it over. The milk flooded the countertop and dripped onto the floor, which wasn't a huge deal since one of our four dogs, Spartacus, came over and started licking it up.

Meanwhile, my second-oldest daughter was sitting at the kitchen table, multitasking. She was eating breakfast and posting a photo of my award-winning breakfast on her Instagram account. All while yelling out across the kitchen for my computer password so she could log in and finish the homework she should have completed the night before.

At the same time, my oldest was nowhere to be found.

It turned out the girl was still in bed, and we had to leave for school in a matter of minutes.

So, with one kid still sleeping, I was helping Brooks clean up his spill with one hand, flipping pancakes with the other, and yelling out my computer password over the barking of another dog who was now peeing on the kitchen floor because no one had let him outside.

Amid this chaos, my youngest daughter yelled out from the bathroom at the top of her lungs, *"More toilet paper!"*

Complete chaos. I had to laugh.

And in that moment, I realized just how needy my children are. As a father, I had to learn quickly that children have numerous needs ...They do!

But, so do we grown-ups, too. Don't we?

And the crazier life gets, the more needs we have. We all have, and will have, different needs according to our context, yet we all have one common universal need.

It's a need we all share and one that we cannot meet on our own: the need for spiritual wholeness.

This is the human condition.

Even though we've been created in the *Image of God*, sin has tainted our good image. It has punctured a hole in our soul.

And because sin has punctured a hole in our soul, we are all left with a vacuum, a void, a gap within that we cannot fill on our own, no matter how much we try.

As human beings, we've tried very hard to fill that hole.

Some of the most brilliant thinkers in history verify this. They have identified this universal human condition—the need for spiritual wholeness—and proposed their own key to addressing this problem.

The ancient Greek philosophers, such as Aristotle, believed that the human void within could be filled through the pursuit and achievement of eudaimonia, which is often translated as happiness.

The first Buddhists believed that spiritual fulfillment could be achieved by living rightly and in harmony with the universe.

The early Confucianists said, "If you can escape from evil by training your mind to think no evil, then you will receive spiritual satisfaction."

Rationalists said that reason (the mind/thinking) is the be-all and end-all for human significance.

For empiricists, the mind and reason aren't enough. Only experiences through the senses can direct a life to purpose and peace within.

The first existentialists were on a quest for ultimate knowledge. But, for them, enlightenment of the soul was next to impossible. So, if you're an existentialist looking for purpose, don't hold your breath. It's not coming.

Materialists point to physical things and possessions as the solution to fill the gap in the human heart and bring meaning to life.

These philosophies are just a few examples of the types of thinking that verify the fact that human beings have always known, or have sensed, within themselves that something is missing.

All of these philosophies attempt, and some of them do a decent job at it, to provide a way to fill the void, the vacuum, the gap within the human soul, and give it purpose.

All of these perspectives strive so desperately to help humanity achieve spiritual wholeness. Still, none of them leaves us entirely satisfied. They all fall short. But we should still give them an "A" for effort.

EXPERIENCING A SPIRITUAL REBIRTH

We should give Nicodemus an "A" for effort as well. It appears that he also worked diligently throughout his life to find a solution to the human condition. Want proof?

Look at his life. Nicodemus is a Pharisee, an expert in Hebrew law. He has wealth, power, and prestige. He's extremely educated, so he's up to speed on the latest and greatest intellectual ideas for finding human significance.

Yet he doesn't appear to be satisfied with the current philosophical solutions to his problem, to the human condition.

He seems to understand that reason, knowledge, happiness, harmony with the universe, positive thinking, stuff, and even righteous living aren't enough to make him whole.

Nicodemus is a man who has a lot and knows a lot, but still feels incomplete.

Even though he's been doing this religion thing for years and has tried his best to live a good, righteous life, nothing he's done up until this night has been good enough to bring him peace.

So he's restless. He has needs.

He needs answers or an answer.

He's looking for more. He's searching for truth. He's on a quest for meaning, significance, and purpose. He's longing for spiritual wholeness. And his restlessness moves him to action.

He's been listening to the buzz about Jesus for a while now. He's had an eye on Him, having seen Jesus in action, watched Him work, and heard Him speak. He knows Jesus is *the Life of the Party* wherever He goes.

Nicodemus begins to wonder, *Who is this guy? Who is this Jesus? Is he for real? Does he really know what he's talking about?*

So, Nicodemus makes his move.

He doesn't even try to fight the craziness of the crowds. He goes to Jesus at night to get some alone time, some quiet, face-to-face time with Jesus, away from the masses and even the disciples. And what happens?

Nicodemus sits down next to Jesus on a large, cold rock or some wooden stool and has the most meaningful conversation of his entire life.

In this conversation, Jesus offers Nicodemus the solution to the human condition.

Jesus tells him that if you want to be whole or complete, "You must... You must be born again."

Can you imagine Nicodemus's initial thoughts after hearing this? He had to be thinking, *Come on, Jesus! Are you for real? What does this even mean? I'm finally told how to become spiritually whole, and it involves something that is obviously impossible to do! Become born again? I don't even get it. What does it mean to be born again, born from above, born of the Spirit? I don't know what you're talking about, Jesus.*

Nicodemus doesn't understand what Jesus is talking about, and Jesus knows that he doesn't.

Jesus breaks it down for Nicodemus and tells him how to be born again. How to come into the kingdom of God. How to get meaning, significance, and purpose. How to receive eternal life and achieve spiritual wholeness.

And how does Jesus do this?

Jesus looks at Nicodemus and says, "For God so loved the world, that he gave his only Son, that whoever believes in him may not perish but have eternal life."

In other words, Jesus tells Nicodemus that if he's looking to fill the void within his soul—if he's looking to be made spiritually whole—then he needs him.

He needs the Son of God.

He needs *the Life of the Party*—the One who is the Way and the Truth and the Life.

He needs a relationship with God in the flesh. He needs Jesus.

Now, does Nicodemus get this?

Maybe not in the moment, but down life's road, I think he does.

In this story, Nicodemus left Jesus that night, probably still a bit in the dark and a little confused. However, it appears that Nicodemus eventually stepped into the light.

John tells us in chapter 7 that Nicodemus stood up for Jesus after Jesus was arrested. In chapter 19, John reports that after Jesus died, Nicodemus was with Joseph of Arimathea the day he went up to Pilate and said, "Give me Jesus... give me his body."

This was a bold move, especially for Nicodemus.

So, based on Nicodemus' extremely bold actions, it is possible that Nicodemus eventually came to realize the need for Jesus.

I'm not sure if Nicodemus came to the conclusion that he needed Jesus, but I do know this: we all need Jesus.

We all do.

Because every one of us is incomplete without him. Without Jesus, we are:

- Unfulfilled.
- Searching for meaning, significance, and purpose.
- In need of spiritual rest and renewal.
- Longing for spiritual healing, wholeness, and strength.

And this is why every one of us needs Jesus.

You need Jesus. I need Jesus.

And here's the good news: right now, through the power of the Holy Spirit, Jesus wants to come into our lives, sit on the throne of our hearts, and *make us whole.*

Jesus wants to make us whole. That's why He came to Earth. That's why He suffered and died. That's why He rose from the grave and conquered sin and death. That's why He sent us the Holy Spirit.

So we can be born again, born of the Spirit, born from above.

So we can have the void, the vacuum, the gap within our souls completely filled.

So we can have the spiritual wholeness we're looking for, the spiritual wholeness we need.

We want this. Right?

We want the empty places of our lives filled with the power and presence of God, don't we? Of course, we do!

And all we have to do is become like little children, as Jesus says in Matthew 18, and admit to God the Father that we desperately *need* God the Son. Then invite Him to come into our lives and live in us through the power of the Holy Spirit.

Now, this isn't just a one-time invitation. It's not only a one-time event. We don't just need Jesus on the day we ask Jesus to repair the hole in our lives.

We need Jesus every single day of our lives, because one day without Him is an empty one.

Spiritual wholeness is a process that begins when we first come to Jesus and continues as we remain in a relationship with Him.

By going to Jesus daily, by arranging some face-to-face time, one-on-one time, alone time with *the Life of the Party* away from the crowds, away from technology, and away from the craziness in our lives.

Because no matter what we have going on, we need Jesus every day. And every day, we need Him more.

I know I need Him. Without Jesus, I can do nothing. I need daily contact with Him, through the power of the Holy Spirit.

I need His love, His peace, His wisdom, His joy, His strength, and His life poured into me each day so I can be the husband, father, and pastor He wants me to be.

My prayer every day of my life is a simple one that comes from a great hymn of the church:

> *In the morning, when I rise.*
> *In the morning, when I rise.*
> *In the morning, when I rise.*
> *Give me Jesus.*
> *Give me Jesus.*
> *Give me Jesus.*
> *You can have the whole world.*
> *Give me Jesus.*

Let's make "Give me Jesus" our prayer, not just today but every day, because only Jesus can fill the empty places and spaces in our lives.

THOUGHT-PROVOKING PARTY FOOD

1. Over the centuries, people have sought something that would bring them satisfaction. What are you searching for?

2. What do you think Nicodemus was searching for?

3. Jesus tells Nicodemus that he won't see the Kingdom of God unless he becomes "born again." When you think about being born again, what comes to your mind?

4. How does Jesus explain the difference between physical birth and spiritual birth?

5. To be born again is more than a once-in-a-lifetime experience. How do we experience daily rebirth?

Now Jesus learned that the Pharisees had heard that he was gaining and baptizing more disciples than John—although in fact it was not Jesus who baptized, but his disciples. So he left Judea and went back once more to Galilee. Now he had to go through Samaria. So he came to a town in Samaria called Sychar, near the plot of ground Jacob had given to his son Joseph. Jacob's well was there, and Jesus, tired as he was from the journey, sat down by the well. It was about noon. When a Samaritan woman came to draw water, Jesus said to her, "Will you give me a drink?" (His disciples had gone into the town to buy food.)

The Samaritan woman said to him, "You are a Jew and I am a Samaritan woman. How can you ask me for a drink?" (For Jews do not associate with Samaritans.)

Jesus answered her, "If you knew the gift of God and who it is that asks you for a drink, you would have asked him and he would have given you living water."

"Sir," the woman said, "you have nothing to draw with and the well is deep. Where can you get this living water? Are you greater than our father Jacob, who gave us the well and drank from it himself, as did also his sons and his livestock?"

Jesus answered, "Everyone who drinks this water will be thirsty again, but whoever drinks the water I give them will never thirst. Indeed, the water I give them will become in them a spring of water welling up to eternal life."

The woman said to him, "Sir, give me this water so that I won't get thirsty and have to keep coming here to draw water."

He told her, "Go, call your husband and come back."

"I have no husband," she replied.

Jesus said to her, "You are right when you say you have no husband. The fact is, you have had five husbands, and the man you now have is not your husband. What you have just said is quite true."

"Sir," the woman said, "I can see that you are a prophet. Our ancestors worshiped on this mountain, but you Jews claim that the place where we must worship is in Jerusalem."

"Woman," Jesus replied, "believe me, a time is coming when you will worship the Father neither on this mountain nor in Jerusalem. You

(cont'd next page)

Samaritans worship what you do not know; we worship what we know, for salvation is from the Jews. Yet a time is coming and has now come when the true worshipers will worship the Father in the Spirit and in truth, for they are the kind of worshipers the Father seeks. God is spirit, and his worshipers must worship in the Spirit and in truth."

The woman said, "I know that Messiah (called Christ) is coming. When he comes, he will explain everything to us."

Then Jesus declared, "I, the one speaking to you—I am he."

Just then his disciples returned and were surprised to find him talking with a woman. But no one asked, "What do you want?" or "Why are you talking with her?" Then, leaving her water jar, the woman went back to the town and said to the people, "Come, see a man who told me everything I ever did. Could this be the Messiah?" They came out of the town and made their way toward him.

Meanwhile his disciples urged him, "Rabbi, eat something."

But he said to them, "I have food to eat that you know nothing about."

Then his disciples said to each other, "Could someone have brought him food?"

"My food," said Jesus, "is to do the will of him who sent me and to finish his work. Don't you have a saying, 'It's still four months until harvest'? I tell you, open your eyes and look at the fields! They are ripe for harvest. Even now the one who reaps draws a wage and harvests a crop for eternal life, so that the sower and the reaper may be glad together. Thus the saying 'One sows and another reaps' is true. I sent you to reap what you have not worked for. Others have done the hard work, and you have reaped the benefits of their labor."

Many of the Samaritans from that town believed in him because of the woman's testimony, "He told me everything I ever did." So when the Samaritans came to him, they urged him to stay with them, and he stayed two days. And because of his words many more became believers.

They said to the woman, "We no longer believe just because of what you said; now we have heard for ourselves, and we know that this man really is the Savior of the world."

JOHN 4:1-42

—CHAPTER 4—
Travel Party

MY GRANDPARENTS were farmers in Wisconsin, and all their water came from a well. They had a pump, so they did have indoor plumbing. But if we were out in the yard on a hot summer day, which is somewhat rare in Wisconsin, and we wanted a drink of water, we had to walk over to the pump and start cranking. Good times!

I have many great childhood memories of that farm, and I loved spending time with my grandfather, Grandpa Nelson.

Grandpa would take my brothers, cousins, and me fishing.

He'd take us on coffee breaks, which were really more like donut breaks.

He'd let us ride with him on the tractor and drive us around on the lawn mower.

We were very active grandkids, but Grandpa was never too tired for us and always kept up with us.

Even when we got older, he'd play half-court basketball with us out in the driveway. He was strong and athletic. And Grandpa was very competitive.

When I was in high school, Grandpa would take us to the park for batting practice. My grandpa would step up to the plate and hit my fastballs over the fence. At age seventy, he could crush me in arm wrestling. And let me tell you, there's nothing more humbling for a sixteen-year-old varsity quarterback than to be beaten by his grandfather in arm wrestling.

My grandfather was a big, strong man, yet so gentle, calm, and Christlike. I loved that man, and I enjoyed spending time with him on the Nelson farm. I loved everything about that farm, except the water.

I did not like the water. It tasted weird, and it smelled bad.

The water I was used to drinking came from Lake Michigan. In my mind, good water should not have a taste or a smell. Grandpa's well water tasted like iron and smelled like rotten eggs, reminiscent of sulfur.

But that's well water for you. It's always refreshingly cold, but unless you're accustomed to it or have a filtering system, it will have an awkward taste and an interesting smell.

So, when I hear Jesus ask the Samaritan woman for a drink from the well, my initial reaction is, *Uh, why? Out of all the places to drink, Jesus, why here? Why stop at this well, Jesus? Why even come to Samaria at all? And besides, don't You have some more of that wine You made back in Cana when You showed everyone there that You are the Life of the Party? Can't You just turn that wine back into water?"*

I don't know why anyone would want to go out of their way to drink water from this source.

See, just like everyone else in the area at this time, Jesus knows that the water in this well is considered dead water.

Sure, it's potable, but it's certainly not the best drinking water around. Nobody alive at that time would have called this well water "living water."

To them, living water was moving water. It was flowing water.

Living water is water that comes from a spring or from a river, like the Jordan. So why in the world would Jesus want to drink from this well?

I don't believe He really does. This story isn't about the well.

TAKING THE ROAD LESS TRAVELED

Sure, the well has significance within the story. It's a key prop, and because it's Jacob's well, its importance is elevated a bit. Jacob's well represents the covenant relationship between God and Jacob's descendants, God's people.

However, this story isn't about the well, nor is it about the woman at the well. Yes, she is a primary character in the story. She's important. She matters.

She gets to hang out with *the Life of the Party*. She gets to have a little talk with Jesus.

And it's the most significant conversation she will ever have, but this story isn't about her, really. Like any other story featuring Jesus, this story is about Him. It's about Jesus.

And when we shift our attention to Him, several profound truths emerge.

The first truth: Jesus is purposeful. He's strategic.

News flash. Jesus knows what He's doing and moves according to the will of God the Father in heaven.

No one can force or coerce Jesus into doing something He doesn't want to do.

Nothing can move Jesus unless He wants to be moved.

He isn't controlled by the circumstances around Him or caught up in the trajectory of the moment. Jesus isn't blown here and there by the wind. He controls the wind, which is why it initially seems so odd when John tells us in verse 4 that Jesus "had to go through Samaria."

He *had* to?

What? That doesn't make sense. Jesus doesn't have to do anything. So what does John mean here?

Well, at the beginning of our story, John mentions the Pharisees. It seems like they're working hard, like they always do, to discredit Jesus and this new movement He has started.

They certainly don't like Jesus' popularity. The Pharisees want to be *the Life of the Party*.

Could it be, then, that Jesus had to go through Samaria because he was afraid to confront these dominant religious leaders? Please.

No way. If you recall, not long before this story, Jesus caused quite a stir in the temple courts when He saw it being used as a marketplace. He drove out sheep and cattle, overturned tables, and scattered coins everywhere—while the Pharisees were watching from their box seats.

Jesus didn't *have to* go to Samaria, because He was not afraid of confrontation or fearful of death. This is the man who says in John 10:18, *"No one takes my life from me, but I lay it down of my own accord."*

At the beginning of our story today, we're also told that Jesus' disciples were baptizing more people than John the Baptist. So maybe Jesus had to go through Samaria because He didn't want to upset John the Baptist.

Could that be it? I don't think so.

John is likely celebrating the fact that more people are flocking to Jesus. This isn't a competition, and John knows it. This is kingdom work.

And just like any other kingdom worker, John's job, in his own words, is "to prepare the way of the Lord."

Jesus doesn't have to go to Samaria because He's outshining John, who was the life of the party before Jesus arrived.

Jesus is the light of the world. He's going to outshine everybody, which is exactly what John the Baptist wants.

And this isn't a matter of geography. Jesus doesn't have to go through Samaria to get from Judea to Galilee. There are alternative routes to travel between these two regions that do not require passing through Samaria.

In fact, traveling Jews wouldn't even go near Samaria because they believed that Samaritans were unclean.

Jesus' path to Samaria was one no other Jew would take. Yet, He took it.

Why? Because if there's anything that drives Jesus, it's His compassion for the hurting and His love for humanity.

Jesus had to go through Samaria because He wanted to go through Samaria.

He had one goal in mind: to bring real life to the people in Samaria.

Jesus went there with a purpose: to bring God's gift of love and hope to a people who were lost and unloved.

That's why Jesus *had* to go through Samaria.

That's why He took the road less traveled.

That's why He took the scenic route, that's why He went out of the way, that's why He purposefully went to the cross, and that's why He still moves throughout this world today—to transform dead water into living water.

This is the gospel. This is good news.

There's a lot of talk nowadays about purpose, wouldn't you agree? Countless books are written, designed to help us somehow, someway find our meaning, significance, and purpose in life. Those books have their place and can be helpful. As we explored earlier, Nicodemus likely has a few books like these in his library.

However, the downside to this pursuit of purpose is that it tends to cause us to think more about our own purposes rather than focusing on God's purposes.

This approach pursues purpose from the bottom up, rather than from the top down, from us to God.

Jesus is purposeful, which means that even now, He is intentionally moving throughout this world with a purpose—to pour the life, love, and hope of God into the hearts of all those who believe in Him.

So instead of praying, "God, help me find *my* purpose in life," let's join together and pray, "Jesus, fulfill *Your* purpose in me. Plant the fullness of *Your* love within me."

Jesus purposely moves the way He moves in our lives because, as we can see from this story, Jesus is personal.

Unlike most people of the time, Jesus wants to go through Samaria. Unlike these religious leaders of the day, Jesus welcomes an encounter with a Samaritan. Unlike these men, Jesus values this woman and speaks with her.

Jesus sits down by this well because He's been traveling all day long. He needs to rest.

I can imagine that His muscles burn a bit. His feet are sore. Maybe He has a nagging ache in his lower back.

He has to be tired, but not too tired. Jesus, *the Life of the Party*, is never too tired for others.

QUENCHED BY THE LIVING WATER

Jesus initiates a conversation with a Samaritan woman, and it's profound. In this brief conversation, Jesus personally reveals His divinity to this woman and displays supernatural knowledge.

Read the rest of the story, and you'll see that Jesus already knows about her past before she even speaks about it.

Jesus knows who she is. He knows her secrets. He knows her culturally constructed feelings of inferiority and insecurity. He knows she feels like an outcast who also feels as though she's outside of God's promises.

Jesus knows what this woman hopes for when she wakes up each day and makes her way over to Jacob's well, and He knows what she dreams about when she lies down each night and gazes up at the heavens.

Jesus knows her most intimate thoughts. He knows the content of her prayers.

In her mind, they just met, but in Jesus' mind, in the mind of God in Christ, she's another beautiful creation of His who is in desperate need of His voice of grace.

In the course of another brief conversation, Jesus graciously conveys this wonderful reality as well. He wants to be her Savior; He wants to be her friend.

While sitting on the wall of this well, Jesus begins to establish a personal relationship with this woman, so that she can come to know just how much she is valued, cherished, and loved by God.

It's such a privilege to watch Jesus at work.

In this story at Jacob's well, we see Jesus do exactly what He came to do: build relationships with people so that they might be brought into the kingdom of God.

Jesus, God wrapped in human flesh, descended to earth, took on flesh and blood, and worked hard to form relationships with others so that they could know God in a personal way.

And Jesus is still working today.

He is not some aloof and distant king who resides in some ivory tower in a kingdom far, far away. He is an ever-present King.

He is Emmanuel, God with us, and through the power of the Holy Spirit, Jesus is present and wants a personal relationship with you and with me. He wants to be our Savior. He wants to be our friend no matter who we are, where we come from, or what we've done.

He isn't just *the Life of the Party*, but He's inviting us to attend the greatest party ever.

His party.

And as our friend, Jesus is never too tired to talk, never too tired to pour His love and hope into our lives, never too tired to meet, and never too tired to make us an everyday priority.

Jesus is serious about having a personal relationship with you and with me. He wants to spend time with us on a daily basis.

I pray each of you has his or her own well that you walk to every day of the week. Somewhere you go to meet Jesus—a quiet space where the two of you can sit and chat.

I hope you have a place where you can go to have a quiet conversation with Jesus and deepen your personal relationship with Him.

Jesus is purposeful. Jesus is personal. And Jesus is powerful.

The woman at the well is expecting Jesus to do the miraculous, but the miracle she's expecting wouldn't have changed her life. She's expecting Jesus to give her living water, moving water, spring water that she can physically drink, even though He's sitting next to a well of stagnant water.

And Jesus could have very easily done what she was expecting, don't you think? After all, this is Jesus we're talking about. The One who created the waters as God in Genesis, along with God the Father and God the Holy Spirit.

He's the One who turned water into wine in Cana, who calmed a sea of water in Galilee, and who walked on water to His disciples.

Water, like the rest of creation, submits to His command and bows to His power. Jesus could turn the Samaritan's well water into the purest water possible or create living water out of nothing, but He doesn't.

Instead, He does something even more miraculous.

Jesus does something even more powerful. He offers the woman something only God can give: eternal life. He offers her spiritual water—water you cannot find in any river, spring, fountain, or well.

My grandparents sold their farm to my aunt and uncle when I was in college and then moved into the two-bedroom apartment above the old farmhouse. It was around that time that Grandpa Nelson was diagnosed with Parkinson's disease.

As you can imagine, within a few years, he was no longer able to do the things he used to do with his grandkids. No more half-court basketball in the driveway, no more batting practice at the park, and no more arm wrestling.

We still took coffee breaks, which were a lot more expensive than when we were little, since each of his grandsons could easily eat a dozen donuts in one sitting.

For a while, we were still able to walk with Grandpa to the pond so he could watch us fish, but in time, even walking became a challenge for him.

I hated what this disease was doing to him, and I was mad—mad at this disease, mad at life, and mad at God. Watching your hero's body and mind break down right before your eyes is an awful experience.

A year after I graduated from college, my grandmother called me one Saturday evening. She asked if I would come over to the house to help Grandpa up the stairs to their apartment.

At the time, I lived only a few miles away, so I got in my car and drove over to the farm. He couldn't get up the first step.

So I took off my coat, picked my grandfather up, and carried him up the stairs—one of the most emotionally difficult things I've ever done.

It wasn't long after that when we had to take Grandpa to the hospital. He couldn't eat on his own, and eventually, he couldn't even drink water on his own.

Water is often something we take for granted, but the reality is that the body cannot survive without water. Of course, he was given fluids through an IV, but that became pointless as his organs began shutting down one by one.

My grandfather's body gave up on him in May 2000 at the age of seventy-seven, but his Savior did not. The Bible tells us that Jesus has the power to give eternal life to a thirsty soul and to raise the dead.

Today, I am convinced with every ounce of my being that my grandfather is more alive than ever before—because he placed his faith in Jesus Christ, and because he drank the living water that Jesus offered him. This is the water He offers us.

And I believe with all my heart that on the day Jesus returns in all His glory, the dead in Christ will rise and my grandpa's living soul will once again be reunited with his resurrected body.

And when that happens, Grandpa will be bigger and stronger than he has ever been.

Our bodies need water.

They were created to thirst for water. And so were our souls.

Every human soul is thirsty. We are either going to drink ourselves to death by taking in the dead water from the well of this world, or we are going to experience life to the fullest by gulping down the living water that Jesus offers.

If you're tired of drinking dead water, then go to Jesus and pray this simple prayer: "Jesus, I believe in you! Please forgive me of my sins, come into my life as my Savior and my friend, and fill me with the living water that gives eternal life."

If you've already tasted the living water Jesus offers, then every time you drink a glass of water, think of this passage and think of Jesus, the One who is purposeful, personal, and powerful.

Be reminded of the supernatural life that flows in you and through you.

Embrace His hope in the face of death.

Share the good news about Jesus, including who He is and what He offers us.

And recite or sing this song that my grandfather sang to me when I was a child:

> *I've got a river of life flowing out of me.*
> *Makes the lame to walk and the blind to see.*
> *Opens prison doors, sets the captive free.*
> *I've got a river of life flowing out of me.*

Take a drink of water today, and praise God that your soul will never, ever thirst again.

THOUGHT-PROVOKING PARTY FOOD

1. When was the last time you were really thirsty?

2. Why do you think Jesus uses "water" and "thirst" to explain a spiritual truth?

3. How does Jesus redirect the conversation with his Samaritan woman?

4. What are the results?

5. What is the "River of Life" and how can it flow through you?

Some time later, Jesus went up to Jerusalem for one of the Jewish festivals. Now there is in Jerusalem near the Sheep Gate a pool, which in Aramaic is called Bethesda and which is surrounded by five covered colonnades. Here a great number of disabled people used to lie—the blind, the lame, the paralyzed. One who was there had been an invalid for thirty-eight years. When Jesus saw him lying there and learned that he had been in this condition for a long time, he asked him, "Do you want to get well?"

"Sir," the invalid replied, "I have no one to help me into the pool when the water is stirred. While I am trying to get in, someone else goes down ahead of me."

Then Jesus said to him, "Get up! Pick up your mat and walk." At once the man was cured; he picked up his mat and walked. The day on which this took place was a Sabbath...

JOHN 5:1-9

—CHAPTER 5—
Pool Party

THERE IS A LOT of excitement in this story, at least at the end when *the Life of the Party* does something amazing again.

But at the start of the story, not so much. It's pretty uneventful at first.

For the people in this passage, the day begins with very little excitement, which is understandable. After all, it's the Sabbath.

And you know what that means, right?

It's the one day of the week when rest is mandatory, according to Jewish law. If you're a Hebrew person living at this time, you're not supposed to exert a lot of energy on this day. You're not allowed to be productive. You can't be caught carrying anything of size in your arms, on your shoulders, or on your head, because that would mean that you are working, which would mean that you are violating the law.

The way I see it, you have only one option on the Sabbath in this setting: to kick back and relax. And in my mind, there's no better place to kick back and relax than beside a pool.

My family and I love hanging around our little pool, especially on hot summer days in Texas.

And we love having friends over for a pool party. We look for excuses to bask in the sun and splash in the water, with a cold drink in our hands and country music playing in the background.

As a family, we also enjoy playing games in the pool, like Marco Polo and volleyball. Every now and then, we'll have a family cannonball contest—more good times.

But for me, it doesn't really matter what we do. I like hanging around the pool with not a care in the world, especially after church on a Sunday afternoon.

So, if I'm living during the time of this story and it's the Sabbath, and I'm supposed to be unproductive, then I'll grab a little piece of paradise next to some clear, cool water and work *really* hard at resting.

But that's just me. That's what I would do on the Sabbath. That's where I would go. The poolside would be my destination if I were required to rest.

Lying out in the sun, with my family playing and laughing all around me, in my mind, is a perfect Sabbath. That's my kind of day of rest!

THE FUTILITY OF WORK

But this kind of Sabbath day isn't a reality for the people who are poolside in this passage. Yes, many people are hanging around the pool, but they're not relaxing. They're not playing games in the water or having a cannonball contest. This is no pool party.

Yes, it's the Sabbath, and they're required to rest, according to the law, but they're not resting. In fact, they're restless.

It's the Sabbath, and they're not supposed to be working—but they are! They're working extremely hard to:

- Survive and stay alive.
- Get and maintain hope.

- Wait for a miracle and watch for a supernatural movement in the water, so they can be the first to take a dip in this ancient fountain of youth.

The people in this story believe that the pool they're lying beside has the potential to receive and give off some sort of mystical, magical healing power.

There are many people gathered around the pool, but they're not relaxing.

The cold, hard, dirty ground they're lying on is certainly no piece of paradise. It's a place of pain: emotional, spiritual, psychological, and for some, physical pain.

Society has ignored and neglected them. Some of their families are embarrassed by and have abandoned them. Life has knocked them down and trampled upon them.

The water in this pool is now taunting them. *Maybe today's your day.* The water seems to say, "If you're lucky."

Luck! That's what many people around the pool are really hoping for, right? They're hoping for luck. But one man no longer hopes for luck. His story, up to this point, is an unpleasant one.

He's been sick for a long time. He knows there's no such thing as luck. He's put his faith in luck for far too long. In his mind, life is what it is: painful, cruel, and pointless.

After thirty-eight years, he believes that hope is fictitious and any notion of healing is ridiculous. For him, it really doesn't matter what day of the week it is. Sabbath Day or not, he's going to do what he has always done: lie despondently upon his mat and simply exist.

Can you see this man with your mind's eye? Can you picture him there upon his mat of despair?

Unfortunately, this isn't just an ancient-day scenario, is it?

There are many people today who are basically doing the same sort of thing as the sick man in this passage. They are lying, metaphorically speaking, on a mat of despair and simply existing.

There are many people all around us who are like those hanging around this ancient-day pool. They are working hard to survive; working hard to stay alive; working hard to get and maintain hope, and working hard to wait for a miracle from some source of fictitious hope.

They're hurting and helpless, neglected and needy, and forsaken and forgotten. They're waiting to catch a break, longing for luck to bail them out, and hoping for life to be merciful to them, since so many in society are not. They have an illness or depression. They have been abused or oppressed. They have lost friends or family members to death.

These hurting people in our world today are at the end of their rope, at the end of their hope. And every day, especially the Sabbath, is just a blur to them, a constant reminder that the waters in their lives are not stirring at all.

But as John reminds us in his Gospel, the waters don't need to move at all for hope to be restored. This story proves beyond a shadow of a doubt that the pools of life don't need to be stirred one bit in order for life to flourish.

John reminds us in his Gospel that there is One who not only created the waters but who is Himself the source of living water. John reminds us that life dwells in Him and flows through Him because He is the Word, the essence of life. He is God wrapped in flesh. He is Jesus. And all the fullness of God dwells in Him.

In this story, John shows us how Jesus has a propensity to mingle with the masses. He's always hanging around those who are in desperate need of a divine touch.

Yes, it's the Sabbath. Yes, it's a mandatory day of rest, a day to refrain from work. But as we can see in this passage, God's work of love never ends. Since Jesus is God in the flesh, His work of love never ends either.

So, Jesus rolls up His sleeves on the Sabbath and gets to work. And why can Jesus work on the Sabbath? By whose authority is He allowed to work on this day? His own authority.

> For the Son of Man is Lord of the Sabbath.
> **MATTHEW 12:8**

He walks with authority and power. He walks with purpose. He approaches this despondent man on the mat and says, "Do you want to get well?"

Well?

Well, this is a surprising and puzzling question, isn't it?

I mean, I don't know about you, but at this point in the story, I'm thinking, *Come on, Jesus. What kind of question is that? Of course, he does. Of course, he wants to get well. The man has been sick for thirty-eight years, Jesus. The answer has got to be yes!*

But the man doesn't answer yes to Jesus' question, does he? Did you notice that?

Instead, this man on his mat looks right past Jesus, like so many people do today, to the stale and stagnant water behind Jesus and says, "I can't get to the water. Every time it bubbles up, I try to get to it, but someone always gets there first."

Obviously, this answer works for Jesus. It's close enough.

It's good enough for Jesus because Jesus knows that this man's heart longs for hope and healing. In this moment, Jesus is moved with compassion and compelled by love.

Then, to ensure that the man on the mat would know that the water in the pool next to him had absolutely nothing to do with his healing, Jesus heals him by simply speaking.

Jesus, the Word of God in flesh, utters a few words, and immediately this man is given complete relief from his sickness and rest for his soul.

Jesus says, "Get up!" The grace of God in Christ is poured upon this man, and immediately, he receives *his* Sabbath.

After this miraculous moment, he walks away from Jesus with a pep in his step and an incredible story to tell.

What a great story! And what a great picture John paints for us of who Jesus is, what Jesus did, and what Jesus can do.

DO YOU WANT TO GET WELL?

Through the power of the Holy Spirit, this same Jesus still walks among humanity, among those who are hurting and helpless, and with those who are discarded and disregarded by society.

This same Jesus is still hanging around those who are in desperate need of His divine touch. This same Jesus still offers healing and wholeness to the afflicted and despondent. This same Jesus still offers Sabbath rest to the restless, regardless of the day of the week.

This same Jesus still walks throughout this world with authority, power, and purpose.

This same Jesus is still ready and willing, and lovingly longing, to speak rest, restoration, and renewal into the lives of all those who look up to Him. Just as the man did on his mat.

Maybe the question for some of us today is the same question Jesus asked the man lying on the mat. "Do you want to get well?"

Are you helpless or hurting? Are you discouraged or depressed? Are you anxious or fearful?

Does it ever feel as though you're lying on a mat of despair? Like life has knocked you down and trampled on you?

Does the stress of school, work, or home feel like it's suffocating you? Are you weighed down by unconfessed sin or by guilt and shame?

Does your soul feel like a stagnant, stale pool of water? Do you need His supernatural touch?

Are you longing for Jesus to speak life into your life? Do you need to hear Him say, "Get up!" and then fill you with the power to do so?

Answering "yes" to any of these questions means answering "yes" to the One whispering, "Do you want to get well?" in your soul.

Look up to Jesus in prayer. Take your Bible, open it up, and explore God's Word. Highlight the promises of Christ, and then hold on to His promises as contained in scripture.

In 1 John, Jesus promises forgiveness to anyone who is consumed by sin, guilt, or shame.

If we confess our sins, He is faithful and just and will forgive us our sins and purify us from all unrighteousness.
1 JOHN 1:9

Those struggling with anxiety and fear find relief in Jesus' promise in 1 Peter.

Cast all your anxiety on him because he cares for you.
1 PETER 5:7

In the book of Matthew, Jesus promises rest to those of us who are burdened, burned out, or at a breaking point.

"Come to me, all you who are weary and burdened, and I will give you rest."
MATTHEW 11:28

If you seek forgiveness, freedom, relief, or rest from exhaustion, go to Jesus. And through the power of the Holy Spirit, Jesus—the Living Water—*will* refill, refresh, and renew your soul.

Only Jesus—the Son of God—can stir the waters of new life within you. The pools of this world—ambition, wealth, success, power, promiscuity, or popularity—are stale and stagnant. They're not life-giving; they're life-draining!

Life—new life, real life, abundant life—is only found in one place: the grace of God in Jesus Christ, *the Life of the Party*. And when it comes to the grace of God in Jesus Christ, grace isn't a pool. It's a bottomless ocean.

Annie Johnson Flint experienced the bottomless and unending grace of God in Jesus Christ. She believed with all her heart that Christ alone could stir the waters of new life within her. And because she relied entirely upon the grace of God in Christ, she had quite a story of her own.

Annie was born in Vineland, New Jersey, on Christmas Eve, 1866, to Eldon and Jean Johnson. When she was three years old, her mother died giving birth to her sister. Three years later, Annie's father died from an incurable disease.

She and her sister suddenly found themselves orphaned, yet both were quickly adopted by the Flint family and raised within the Baptist faith tradition.

When Annie was eight years old, she gave her life to Christ. She began expressing her love for her Savior through music and poetry, despite all the heartache she had experienced at such a young age.

As a teenager, Annie developed arthritis. At first, it only affected her ability to write and play the piano, but by the time she was a young adult, she was unable to walk.

Not long after that, both of her adopted parents died within a few months of each other from different incurable diseases, leaving Annie and her sister orphans for a second time. But Annie's faith in God was strong.

Even though she was an orphan in the eyes of the world, she knew she wasn't an orphan since she was a child of God.

People said that she was always optimistic and positive, and that she loved giving to others, often being reluctant to receive. Even though she suffered in many ways throughout her life, she was always mindful of the needs of others and not her own.

Annie dreamed of being a composer and concert pianist.

But her illness got so bad that it eventually deprived her completely of her ability to play the piano at all, so she resorted to writing poetry. Unable to even open her hands because the arthritis was so bad, Annie wrote many of her poems and hymns on the typewriter, using only her knuckles.

In this condition, with joy in her heart, she painfully typed these words:

He giveth more Grace when the burdens grow greater,
He sendeth more strength as the labors increase;
To added afflictions, He addeth His mercy,
To multiplied trials, He multiplies peace.

His love has no limits, His grace has no measure,
His power, no boundary known unto men;
For out of His infinite riches in Jesus
He giveth, and giveth, and giveth again.

Wow! What a testimony to the goodness and grace of God in Jesus Christ.

Annie lived a difficult life in so many ways. She experienced much physical, emotional, and psychological pain. But instead of lying on her mat of despair and despondency, allowing a pool of resentment or hopelessness to gather in her soul, she put her faith in Christ, and she lived with a river of life flowing out of her.

And because she put her faith in Jesus, on the day she died, she heard her Savior say, "Get up and walk," and now she's walking with Jesus down heaven's streets of gold.

Annie had an amazing encounter with *the Life of the Party* and his love. And when we encounter Jesus, when we put our faith in Him, the Lord of the Sabbath and *the Life of the Party*, when we allow Jesus to be the Lord of our lives and spend time with Him every day, we will continue to receive the grace "He giveth and giveth and giveth again."

 **THOUGHT-PROVOKING PARTY FOOD**

1. Why do you think God designed one day of the week as a day of rest (Sabbath)?

2. How good is our world at observing that day? How about you?

3. Why do you think Jesus asked the man, "Do you want to get well?"

4. What role does obedience play in this story?

5. Where do you see yourself in this story?

That day when evening came, he said to his disciples, "Let us go over to the other side." Leaving the crowd behind, they took him along, just as he was, in the boat. There were also other boats with him. A furious squall came up, and the waves broke over the boat, so that it was nearly swamped. Jesus was in the stern, sleeping on a cushion.

The disciples woke him and said to him, "Teacher, don't you care if we drown?"

He got up, rebuked the wind and said to the waves, "Quiet! Be still!"

Then the wind died down and it was completely calm. He said to his disciples, "Why are you so afraid? Do you still have no faith?"

They were terrified and asked each other, "Who is this? Even the wind and the waves obey him!"

MARK 4:35-41

—CHAPTER 6—
Boat Party

JESUS CALMS THE STORM is one of my all-time favorite Bible stories. I love it for several reasons.

It's theologically significant and profound because it highlights both the humanity and the divinity of Jesus. Jesus is fully God and fully human, which is one of the greatest mysteries of our faith. This story lays the mystery of Christ's nature right before our eyes.

At the same time, this story is a simple representation of life, a reflection of reality. The reality is that life can be filled with clear blue skies and calm waters one day, or even one hour, and then be enveloped by dark storm clouds and rough seas the next. This story is really profound and simple.

But I especially love this story because it has latched itself onto my heart.

Out of the hundreds of stories in the Bible, this is the story I have shared with my children the most. So, this story of how Jesus calms the storm has become our story.

It has latched onto their hearts just like it has latched onto mine. My children have come to love it just as much as I do, and that warms my heart.

One of the greatest privileges and joys I have as a father is sharing the Bible with my children and telling them about *the Life of the Party*.

One evening, a few years ago, after all the kids were sufficiently tickled, per our nightly routine, I sent them upstairs to do three simple things: brush their teeth, put on their pajamas, and get into bed.

Nothing complicated, right? Should be easy directions to remember and follow.

A few minutes later, I went upstairs to tuck each of them into bed. My children knew that not only would I tickle them nightly, but they also knew that I would sing them a song, tell them a story, say a prayer, and kiss them each night I was at home.

This particular night, I tucked my older daughters into bed first. Three songs, three stories, three prayers, and three kisses later, I walked into my youngest son's room. I sang Brooks a song and told him a story—this story: *Jesus Calms the Storm*.

We immediately jumped into the story. I mean, we were there. We were in it. We were in the storm with the disciples.

We swayed from side to side, imagining his bed as the boat. We created sound effects for the rain, thunder, and wind. This was Oscar-worthy stuff here, y'all—we were having fun with it! But about halfway through our little reenactment, I noticed something odd.

While replicating the wind, it became evident to me that Brooks had not brushed his teeth, and it *smelled* like he might not have brushed his teeth for quite some time!

Anyway, we continued the story. Jesus calmed the storm, and the disciples were amazed. At the end, we both yelled out dramatically, "Even the wind and the waves obey him!"

In retrospect, my next move was ill-timed, considering the recent storm's calming and the precious moment I had shared with my son. But I had to address his breath and the fact that he didn't obey me when I told him to brush his teeth.

So I looked at him and said, "Brooks, I told you to brush your teeth. Did you brush your teeth?" No response.

He froze, which meant he hadn't brushed his teeth, and there was something else going on.

I pulled back the covers to help him get out of bed so he could brush his teeth. There was a Captain America convention going on under his covers. All the Avengers had assembled in his bed, and he was still in his clothes! No pajamas on—my perfect parenting moment ruined.

Right then and there, Brooks and I had a little "come to Jesus" talk. I said, "Brooks, I told you to brush your teeth and get your pajamas on. Why didn't you obey?"

He said, "'Cuz I was playing." Thank you, Captain Obvious!

I took a deep breath, took his hand, helped him brush his teeth, helped him put on pajamas, helped him back into bed, said a prayer, and kissed his forehead.

Then, to ensure that he learned his lesson, I looked at him and said, "Brooks, who's in charge?"

Without missing a beat, he looked up at me, as serious as he could be, and said, "Jesus."

Of course, he was right. How could I argue with him? It was true.

WHO IS IN CHARGE HERE?

Who's in charge? This is a prevalent question, and not just among assertive parents. This is a common question of authority among all humanity. History and experience show us that, right or wrong, hierarchy and humanity have always held hands.

And they're holding hands in this story.

I can imagine that the question "Who is in charge?" was flooding the minds of the disciples in this passage, on this boat, in the middle of this storm.

I can picture the disciples looking around the boat frantically, squinting at each other through the wind and rain, desperately trying to figure out which one of them will take charge, lead the way, and get them out of this mess.

I can almost hear Matthew saying, "Hey, don't look at me. I don't know anything about sailing. I know about money. I used to collect taxes for a living, so I'm familiar with finances. But we can't buy our way out of this bind."

And then maybe Matthew looked to the seasoned fishermen in the boat, because, after all, they were the ones with all the experience, knowledge, and wisdom needed to step up, take charge, and take control in situations like this, right?

I'm reasonably certain that Andrew, James, and John had navigated rough waters before and had weathered big storms in the past. The reality was that this storm was just too much for them.

Not even Peter—the proven, take-charge leader in the group with a type A personality and a seize-control mentality—could bring them out of this chaos.

This storm had all the elements of the worst storm imaginable; it was complete chaos. It was total turmoil and pure havoc. Here was the perfect storm, and everything about this situation was totally out of their control.

The disciples were being swamped with water. Their little boat was in danger of being crushed by the crashing waves, assuming it didn't sink first from the amount of water in the boat. They were probably bailing out water with their hands or buckets, but in this mess, that was just an exercise in futility.

The disciples in this story, on this boat, in the middle of this storm, really believed they were in danger of drowning. They were shaking with fear. They were terrified out of their minds. So the question, "Who's in charge?" had to have been the question the disciples were asking themselves.

Because they were in a ferocious storm, out in the middle of a large body of water, on a very small wooden boat, and in this chaos, they believed no one was in charge or in control.

THE SEA OF ANXIETY

When there's a belief that no one's in charge or in control, when there's a belief that there's an absence of authority, there will always be an increase in anxiety. And this is where we find the disciples.

They're drowning in a sea of anxiety.

This is where we find many people today, drowning in a sea of anxiety. The chaos of this world, or the chaos in their lives (or both), is causing many people today to shake their heads in disbelief, throw up their hands in desperation, and ask, "Who's in charge?"

- People are looking at the violence, oppression, and injustice around the world and wondering, *Who's in charge?*
- They're watching the economy and wondering, *Who's in charge?*
- They're looking into the political arena or examining the decay of this culture and wondering, *Who's in charge?*
- They're looking at their finances, relationships, or health and wondering, *Who's in charge?*

Many people today are being sucked into a global storm, or they're in the middle of a ferocious personal storm, and the storm has all the elements of the worst storm imaginable.

It's complete chaos. It's total turmoil. It's pure havoc. It's the perfect storm.

We all know what a perfect storm looks like because we've all been in one, metaphorically speaking. Some of you are in one now.

It's a terrifying place to be, isn't it? Because when you're in the middle of extremely chaotic circumstances or severely stressful situations (that are beyond your control), there's a tendency to allow anxiety to chase away your peace and let fear replace your faith.

That's what's happening to the disciples in this passage, on this boat, in this storm. They're allowing anxiety to chase away their peace. They're allowing fear to replace their faith. They had peace and faith on land.

Things were great for them on land.

They heard Jesus teach, and they watched Him work. They saw Him heal the sick and cast out demons. They began to see that Jesus is *the Life of the Party* wherever He is.

Right before this story, they had front-row seats as Jesus taught a massive crowd all about the kingdom of God.

The disciples believed Jesus was in charge and in control, that He had authority on land.

Before this ferocious storm came down upon them, they were probably all smiles, fist-bumping and high-fiving each other, so excited to see what Jesus would do on the other side, on land.

But then the storm hits, on water, and they come unraveled.

You know, it's too bad they couldn't capture the peace they had on land and tap into it while on the water.

It's too bad they couldn't transfer their faith from the land to the boat.

It's too bad they couldn't stop anxiety and fear from taking over their emotions.

Unfortunately, they didn't heed Jesus' words and believe that when He said, "Let us go to the other side!" He meant, "Let us go to the other side!"

It's too bad they didn't know more about this man who was "in the stern sleeping on a pillow" (like verse 38 says).

It's too bad they didn't know then, in the storm, what we know now—that Jesus is the Alpha and Omega, the First and Last, the Lord of Life, Lord of the Harvest, Lord of Creation, Lord of All, *the Life of the Party*, and the Prince of Peace.

It's too bad they didn't really know who Jesus was, because if they really knew who Jesus was, they wouldn't have allowed their circumstances to weaken their faith. They would not have believed that things were actually out of control. But they really didn't know who Jesus was until after the storm.

It took a life-threatening, life-changing experience like this one to teach them two essential truths: Jesus can become so tired that He can sleep through a storm because He's human, and He can command the same storm to calm down because He's God.

In this story, on this boat, in the middle of this storm, the disciples learn *who's in charge*!

Do you think the disciples ever ran from storms after this?

I doubt it. I don't think they ran from storms. Instead, I think they became storm chasers.

BECOMING A STORM CHASER

I can visualize the disciples, weeks or months later, sitting on the shore of the Sea of Galilee, eating salted fish and freshly baked bread. I can picture Peter elbowing James and John after looking out at the horizon. I can hear him say, "Boys, look out there! See that storm? Hey, we've got Jesus, so let's go sailing!"

I can imagine that if they were ever out in a boat again, in the middle of a storm, they would keep calm and carry on because they had Jesus with them.

In 1939, England faced a serious and imminent threat of invasion by Germany. Obviously, this was a serious threat to its national security and to the morale of the English people. During the war, the British government appointed the Ministry of Information to create and distribute a number of morale-boosting posters.

These posters were designed to be displayed throughout England, reminding citizens that they were a steadfast people. Two of these posters were distributed by the thousands, but a third was made and never used.

The third poster read, "KEEP CALM AND CARRY ON."

This third poster was to be issued only if Germany actually invaded. Of course, Germany never did invade, so these posters were never distributed. But isn't this a powerful message?

I love this. I love what it says, and I love what it communicates: "Hey, no matter what comes your way in life, keep calm and carry on."

This statement is a powerful, positive, and persuasive piece of propaganda that can help lead people through times of high anxiety and fear. But if you take these words and place them in the context of our faith, they can become a powerful, positive, and persuasive proclamation!

"KEEP CALM AND CARRY ON" can change from propaganda to proclamation when Jesus is added to the mix. This message can become so much more than a simple statement of positive thinking when it's grounded on the truth that Jesus is in control.

Jesus is *the Life of the Party* wherever He is because He has authority over everything—everything in the physical world and everything in the spiritual world.

And because Jesus is in control, we can be at peace amid chaos. When storms come our way, when adversity confronts us, when anxiety and fear swell around us or within us, we can remain calm and carry on because we know who's in charge.

Within the chaos, we can receive the peace of Christ and bring that peace into the most hostile and anxious of situations.

Ask yourself today, "Do I believe in the authority of Jesus Christ—that He is the Lord of Lords and the Prince of Peace? Do I embrace His promise that He is with me always?"

If you do, if you believe in Jesus—*the Life of the Party*—if you have faith in His power and embrace His promises, then you will have the strength to keep calm and carry on, no matter what obstacles come your way.

You can become a storm chaser.

 **THOUGHT-PROVOKING PARTY FOOD**

1. What situations or circumstances make you anxious?

2. When's the last time an unexpected "storm" caught you by surprise?

3. How does knowing that Jesus is in charge help in your daily life?

4. Knowing that Jesus is in charge, list some ways that you manage to keep calm and carry on.

They left that place and passed through Galilee. Jesus did not want anyone to know where they were, because he was teaching his disciples. He said to them, "The Son of Man is going to be delivered into the hands of men. They will kill him, and after three days he will rise."

But they did not understand what he meant and were afraid to ask him about it. They came to Capernaum. When he was in the house, he asked them, "What were you arguing about on the road?"

But they kept quiet because on the way they had argued about who was the greatest.

Sitting down, Jesus called the Twelve and said, "Anyone who wants to be first must be the very last, and the servant of all."

MARK 9:30-35

—CHAPTER 7—
Royal Party

I LOVE FALL. As a kid growing up in Wisconsin, fall was my favorite time of the year.

On many fall Sundays, my family and I would pick up fried chicken, mashed potatoes and gravy, and honey biscuits on the way home from church. We'd always set up our TV trays in the family room to watch America's team—the Green Bay Packers.

Now, Green Bay wasn't very good in the 1980s (I know that's hard to believe), but we were die-hard fans. Still are!

We got into every game. Not a quarter went by without someone in my family jumping up and down in excitement or yelling at the ref on the TV screen.

Let me tell you that you haven't really watched a football game unless you've watched a Packers game with Packers fans, especially the Nelsons.

After the game, my brothers and I would go outside and toss around the pigskin with our dad. Even my mom and my twelve-year-younger sister joined in on the fun as the years went by.

When I was about six or seven, we used an old football that my dad got as a teenager in the 1960s. Over time, we wore that thing out and eventually replaced it with the one I now have on a shelf in my office. Even that football has been thrown and caught thousands of times, maybe even tens of thousands!

As if it were yesterday, I can still picture my dad patiently corralling his three young rambunctious boys and corralling us with such ease.

We were wild at heart, and we each had quite an imagination.

In our parents' backyard, my brothers and I pretended we were playing in the Super Bowl. We imagined ourselves throwing or catching the game-winning touchdown as the crowd went wild.

Each one of us wanted to grow up and become an NFL superstar. Each one of us wanted to be a Green Bay Packer.

And not only that, when it came to football, each one of us wanted to be the best. We wanted to be great—to achieve greatness. Sometimes, we would even argue which one of us would be the greatest.

WHO IS THE GREATEST?

I can relate very well to the disciples in this story as they argue about the same thing. Maybe you can relate to it, as well. I can imagine walking behind Christ, on the way to Capernaum, alongside His disciples, as they argue about which one of them is the greatest.

Can you imagine their conversation? Can you hear them?

I can hear them arguing about who is the greatest by pointing out who has been with Jesus the longest and who has walked with Jesus the farthest. Or who witnessed *the Life of the Party* doing the most miracles?

And as they're walking down this dusty trail, maybe Andrew makes his case for greatness first. Maybe he says something like, "Hey guys, out of the twelve of us, I believe I'm the greatest because, after all, I'm the one who found the fish and bread, which means I'm the reason Jesus was able to feed over five thousand people."

And then maybe John chimes in, "Hello! Son of Zebedee here. Jesus calls me a Son of Thunder. Thunder equals power, and power equals greatness. Right?"

And you know Peter can't ever keep his mouth shut. So maybe he tries to build a case for being the greatest, too. I can hear Peter say something like, "Hey, guys. Reality check time. Who here, besides Jesus, has walked on water? Oh, that's right. That would be me!"

Regardless of what the disciples may or may not be saying as they walk down this little, dusty trail, their little argument about which one of them is the greatest is not just a matter of competition. They're not trash-talking for fun, at this point.

This isn't some silly game they've made up just to pass the time. They are serious about this!

They're seriously debating which one of them is the greatest, which means they're seriously self-centered, aren't they?

Here's the most disturbing part: Jesus had just told them in verse 31 that he was going to be "betrayed into human hands" and killed.

Jesus just told them he's going to be murdered, and two verses later, we discover that all the disciples were really concerned about was themselves and their status as a disciple.

How embarrassing, right?

Like little kids in the backyard on a Wisconsin fall Sunday afternoon, these grown men, these followers of Christ, are arguing about who is the greatest.

They're obviously not talking about who is the greatest in a particular sport. Their argument goes way beyond the world of sports. They're not talking about who is the greatest fisherman or farmer. No.

Get this: Matthew tells us in Matthew 18 that the disciples are arguing about which one of them is the greatest in the kingdom of heaven.

Wow. You talk about audacious pretentiousness.

Who do these guys think they are? They've been following Jesus for a year or two. So what? Big deal.

What have they really done on their own, up to this point? What have they accomplished, by themselves, for God? Nothing!

Jesus is the One who has been doing all the work. He's the One preaching and teaching with boldness and courage, with wisdom and power and insight. He's the One healing the sick, feeding the hungry, and raising the dead.

Jesus is *the Life of the Party*, not them.

These guys get to learn from the most outstanding teacher ever. They get to walk in the dust of the one and only Son of God. They get to hear the good news—the Word of God—every single day. They have the opportunity to see the lame walk, the blind see, the lepers cleansed, and the storms calmed. Through this opportunity, they have witnessed hundreds of miracles.

These disciples get to walk with God in the flesh, yet they somehow think that because they've been tagging along behind Jesus, walking in Jesus' shadow, and breathing in His dust, that somehow that makes them candidates for greatness.

They seem to think that following Jesus alone qualifies them to be eligible for the consideration of being the greatest person in existence.

Well, it doesn't. That's not how the kingdom works.

They obviously don't understand, and they're focused on the wrong things. Being number one isn't the aim of a true disciple. Being the greatest is not the goal of Christian life.

I know this now, and I know this because, over time, I've learned how to define the term "greatness" properly.

UNDERSTANDING TRUE GREATNESS

As I reflect on those fall Sundays in Wisconsin, playing football in the backyard with my family, I realize that my definition of greatness has been flawed for years.

Thinking back on my life, I also realize that I've attempted to apply the wrong definition of greatness to the Christian faith. And, you just can't do that!

It doesn't work that way, even though the world tries to convince us otherwise.

See, all of us are being bombarded by society with the bogus notion that greatness means being the greatest, that greatness involves a climb to the top.

For the world, greatness is about leaving the masses behind and surpassing everybody else, so that you can prevail with the most accomplishments, the biggest trophies, or the largest and loudest accolades.

These are examples of how the world defines greatness, but it's not at all how Jesus defines it. His definition isn't easy to grasp because it's so antithetical to the world's mindset.

So, how does Jesus define greatness? It's right here, in this story.

Jesus' definition appears to be paradoxical. It seems to contradict itself, but it doesn't because it accurately reflects God's truth and the kingdom of God. The definition of greatness emerges in verse 35 when Jesus says, "Whoever wants to be first [great] must be last of all and servant of all." [Emphasis added]

Greatness, according to Jesus, isn't a goal.

You don't become great by trying to be the greatest or by trying to achieve greatness. Greatness is the natural byproduct of a life lived in complete selflessness and servanthood.

Greatness, according to Jesus, isn't the result of some competition that involves you or me coming out ahead of the pack. Greatness is about serving the pack, especially those at the back. For Jesus, true greatness isn't measured by first-place finishes. It's about the willingness to come in last place for the glory of God and the benefit of others.

Greatness isn't about personal ambition, accomplishments, victories, production, or impressive results. It's about making personal sacrifices for others and loving others more than yourself.

Jesus said greatness isn't about an upward trajectory. It's not an ascent to some level of superiority. Greatness is a descent into pure humility, which is exactly what Jesus did for us.

In Philippians, Paul says our attitude should be the same as that of Christ Jesus. Do you see what happens in the following scripture?

> Who, being in very nature God, did not consider equality with God something to be used to his own advantage; rather, He made Himself nothing by taking the very nature of a servant, being made in human likeness. And being found in appearance as a man, He humbled himself by becoming obedient to death— even death on a cross! Therefore, God exalted Him to the highest place and gave Him the name that is above every name, that at the name of Jesus every knee should bow, in heaven and on earth and under the earth, and every tongue acknowledge that Jesus Christ is Lord, to the glory of God the Father.
> **PHILIPPIANS 2:6-11**

Jesus descended from heaven to humanity, to become a servant who served humanity with His life and then served us with His death and then served us with His life again. And because Jesus served us as He did, God made Him great. Through an attitude of humility, Jesus *descended* into greatness.

It's true that He was already great as God in heaven, as a full and equal member of the Trinity. However, by becoming the ultimate servant, Jesus redefined what it means to be great. He actually and properly defined greatness, making greatness and servanthood synonymous terms.

As a kid tossing the football around on a Sunday afternoon, I was defining greatness, out of incredible naivety, by how the world defines it. Little did I know at the time that the epitome of greatness was standing in the backyard playing catch with me.

It was my dad! Keeping up with three boys likely left him exhausted.

I'm sure he was ready to chill out after a long week's work, sprawl out on the couch, and take a nap. I'm sure that his right arm was probably *really* sore from all the passes he threw, but it didn't matter how he felt. He was outside with us, for us!

Dad wasn't thinking about his own needs, desires, and dreams; he was thinking about us and our needs, desires, and dreams—no matter how exaggerated and far-fetched they were.

Dad was always serving us and always serving others, and to this day, he still does.

He serves his wife, his sons and their wives, and his daughter and her husband. He serves his grandchildren. He serves his sisters, his brother, and all their families. He serves his church. He serves his community. He serves his friends.

Through all my dad's service in these various areas, he serves his King, and he serves like his King.

He's a servant like his Savior in my book, and according to the Bible, that makes him great.

I could say the same thing about my mother and many others in my life, as well as many others in this world. They are people of humility.

True humility, according to an old adage, is *not thinking less of yourself, but thinking of yourself less.*

These people serve like Jesus, without any need for recognition or praise, and that's greatness.

One of the greatest truths that emerges from this passage is that each one of us is called to this kind of greatness. We are called to biblical greatness.

I know I am. I don't just want to be a *good* son; I want to be a *great* one. I don't want to be a good husband. I want to be a great husband.

I'm not going to settle for being a good father. I want to be a great father. This applies equally to my roles as a friend, pastor, and person.

I'm not alone, am I? No. I know you all want to be great, too. And I know that each one of you is called to biblical greatness.

So, aim to be the best friend, person, employee, employer, teacher, student, spouse, and parent you can be. Clothe yourself with humility. Think of yourself less, and become last. Become nothing. Become a servant of all, and through the power of the Holy Spirit, become like Jesus.

Don't try to be the life of the party, but allow *the Life of the Party* to shine through you.

And always remember that greatness is found through our service and is encompassed with humility.

Let Jesus' humility cover you from head to toe, and then go serve Him; serve others; serve your friends, your family, your church, your community, and your country; and serve like Christ would serve.

Serve like Jesus. That's true greatness.

 **THOUGHT-PROVOKING PARTY FOOD**

1. What does "greatness" look like to you?

2. How is Jesus' example of greatness different from the world's definition of greatness?

3. Why do you think humility is such a powerful virtue?

4. James 4:10 teaches that we are to humble ourselves in the sight of the Lord. How is that accomplished?

5. What great things do you want to do for God?

Jesus entered Jericho and was passing through. A man was there by the name of Zacchaeus; he was a chief tax collector and was wealthy. He wanted to see who Jesus was, but because he was short he could not see over the crowd. So he ran ahead and climbed a sycamore-fig tree to see him, since Jesus was coming that way.

When Jesus reached the spot, he looked up and said to him, "Zacchaeus, come down immediately. I must stay at your house today." So he came down at once and welcomed him gladly.

All the people saw this and began to mutter, "He has gone to be the guest of a sinner."

But Zacchaeus stood up and said to the Lord, "Look, Lord! Here and now I give half of my possessions to the poor, and if I have cheated anybody out of anything, I will pay back four times the amount."

Jesus said to him, "Today salvation has come to this house, because this man, too, is a son of Abraham. For the Son of Man came to seek and to save the lost."

LUKE 19:1-10

—CHAPTER 8—
House-Warming Party

I USED TO LOVE climbing trees. During my childhood, climbing trees was a daily part of my summer routine.

There's something special about finding yourself up at the top of a big oak tree where the robins' nest rests and the squirrels play.

In the right tree and with the right landscape, the view is breathtaking.

Plus, you can see so much from a treetop vantage point. That's partly why I'm drawn to this story so much. That's why I understand what Zacchaeus did.

And that's why I invite you now to climb a tree, metaphorically speaking, of course so that we can get a bird's-eye view of this story.

Zacchaeus, an official employee of the Roman Empire, begins his day like he begins all his days.

He leaves his house early in the morning, pushes his way through the crowded streets, arrives at his station a little later than usual, sits down at his tax booth, and starts thinking about where he's going to stack all the different kinds of taxes he's going to collect this day.

To his left, he'll stack the annual poll taxes collected for the day. The Romans referred to this tax as the "*tributum capitis*." All non-Roman citizens between the ages of twelve and sixty-five pay this tax every year just for the privilege of existing. It's a fee to exist.

To his right, he'll stack income taxes. There's not as much room needed in the booth for this tax. It's only about one percent of the person's income. Since the majority of people are poor, this tax is relatively small.

Behind him, at the very back of the booth, he'll place the ground tax collected for the day, which was one-tenth of all grain and one-fifth of all wine and oil that the people owned. He needs a lot more space for this tax, as it can be paid with coins or with the actual amount of grain, wine, and oil owed.

Now, as a tax collector, Zacchaeus is going to receive a percentage of each of these taxes he collects on this day. And because he's a chief tax collector, he's also going to get a cut of the taxes collected by all the tax collectors who report to him. Which partly explains why he's wealthy, as Luke tells us.

But a large part of Zacchaeus's money will come from a different source.

And it's money he will obtain unethically.

Zacchaeus has a special spot nearby for the special taxes, the big taxes. Taxes that Zacchaeus, as an authorized tax collector of Rome, gets to determine himself.

Zacchaeus has the power to create and collect import and export duties. He can create and collect tolls for the use of roads in and out of town. He has the power to impose a tax on almost anything.

He can say, "Hey! Today, I think I'm going to tax people for every donkey they own and bring into town."

He can do that. And he can tax people per cart, per donkey, and even per wheel for every cart and donkey they own. Because Zacchaeus can tax in this way, as he sees fit, it's very easy for him to pocket most of the money he collects from these special taxes.

Rome won't even care, as long as it gets the first three taxes.

But the people care. They know what tax collectors do. The people know what Zacchaeus gets away with. In their eyes, there's minimal distinction, if any, between Zacchaeus and a common thief.

To them, he's an extortionist who can't be trusted.

He's despised and ostracized. Socializing with him is unacceptable. Being his close associate or friend is inexcusable, which means that Zacchaeus has no friends.

He has no friends. He has money. He's surrounded by money—stacks and stacks of money, but he has no friends.

From our bird's-eye view, we can clearly see and understand that, up until the moment Zacchaeus climbs a tree, money is his only friend.

Money is his only love, his life's purpose, his definition of happiness. Money is his ruler.

And because money controls him, because it rules his life, and because it dictates how he lives, it determines the trajectory of his life.

Because money reigns over him with gold and silver fists, it is just as much a tyrant in his life as Caesar is in Rome.

With money seated upon the throne of his heart, there's little room, if any, for God and the things of God. Zacchaeus has allowed money to push God to the perimeters of his existence and maybe even beyond.

At the beginning of this story—before he climbs a tree and comes into contact with the liberating power of Jesus—Zacchaeus is a prime example; he's the poster child for the dichotomy that Jesus talks about in Matthew.

> "No one can serve two masters. Either you will hate the one and love the other, or you will be devoted to the one and despise the other. You cannot serve both God and money."
> **MATTHEW 6:24**

Zacchaeus is living proof of this truth. Money is his lord until Jesus comes to town. When *the Life of the Party* arrives, everything changes.

Because Jesus comes to town, Zacchaeus is drawn to Him. And because Zacchaeus is drawn to Jesus, Zacchaeus becomes desperate to see Him.

Because Zacchaeus becomes desperate to see Jesus, he climbs a tree.

Because he climbs a tree, he hears some good news. He hears the gospel, and he hears Jesus say, "I must come to your house today."

Because he hears Jesus say, "I must come to your house today," he responds willingly. Because he responds willingly, Jesus comes into his home.

Because Jesus comes into his home and makes His way to the center of Zacchaeus's life, "I must come to your house" changes and turns into "salvation has come to this house."

Because salvation has come to this house, the chains of greed that bound Zacchaeus are broken by the One who sets the captives free, and a heavenly party begins.

Zacchaeus does a 180-degree turn. He changes his allegiances. He changes rulers. And he also changes lords.

The tyrant in his life is dethroned, and the myth that money brings purpose and happiness is debunked.

Zacchaeus's life is radically transformed the moment he experiences the liberating presence and power of Jesus. Zacchaeus let Jesus into his house as a guest, but the moment Jesus entered Zacchaeus's house, Zacchaeus became the guest, and Jesus became *the Life of the Party* and the center of his life.

Wow! Who would have dreamed that climbing a tree could be so life-changing? But it is.

When Jesus becomes the center of Zacchaeus's life, everything about Zacchaeus's life changes, especially his relationship to his money. Standing in the presence of *the Life of the Party* allows Zacchaeus to see money differently. One of the first things to change in his life is his perspective on money.

Before Jesus, Zacchaeus saw money as his primary pursuit. It was the prize he sought day after day. It was the goal toward which he aimed his life. Money was his target, but then he met Jesus, and the target became a tool—a tool for helping others, which, in turn, led to a change in his priorities.

The new Zacchaeus, this transformed man, seems to be thinking, *Hey, instead of building a stockpile of wealth for myself, or instead of making myself the number one priority when deciding where my money is spent, I can use my money and possessions as an instrument of grace to help those in need.*

Zacchaeus looks around his life and decides that his wealth is an asset that can be used as a powerful tool to provide for the basic needs of the poor. Zacchaeus embraces Jesus. Money, which was once his goal, becomes a tool because the poor are now Zacchaeus's priority.

What a transformation!

And based upon his desire to make right for all the wrongs he has done, and based upon his longing to pay back "four times the amount" he had cheated out of anybody (to use his words), I believe his business practices changed, too.

Before Jesus, Zacchaeus's business motto was, *Make as much money as possible, by any means necessary,* which is a motto built upon an ancient form of utilitarian thinking.

After Zacchaeus's encounter with Jesus, I'm pretty sure it's safe to say that Zacchaeus went back to work the next day with a new business plan in mind—a plan grounded in righteousness and fairness and justice.

From our bird's-eye view of this passage, we can see that Zacchaeus experiences quite a change. He changes rulers first, from money to Jesus. Then he changes his perspective on money, his priorities for where he spends it, and his business practices for obtaining it. All these changes happened to him because *the Life of the Party* came to town.

Isn't it amazing what you can see when you climb a tree? Aerial views are incredibly beneficial. You can see the big picture so much easier when you're above it and looking down.

So, with this story on the forefront of our minds, let's climb a tree together, one more time, to get a bird's-eye view of money in our context today.

Without much effort, we can all look down at the big picture and see that money is a significant part of our lives.

Money is important. You've gotta have it to pay the bills, to buy the basics, to purchase clothing, to feed the family, to fund endeavors, to make investments, to acquire healthcare, and to support those in need.

Money is meaningful to us today, for sure, because money is something that signifies value.

Money matters to us because we exchange it for things we value; we trade it for the things we treasure. We treasure food, water, clothing, cars, homes, education, and entertainment, so we give money to others—to retailers and suppliers—in exchange for these things, these treasures.

This means that the things we value—our treasures—are closely connected to our money.

Our treasures and our money go hand in hand, so our hearts and our money go hand in hand as well. Read what Jesus said in Luke 12.

For where your treasure is, there your heart will be also.
LUKE 12:34

Since our money is closely tied to our treasures, and our treasures are closely tied to our hearts, our hearts are also closely tied to our money.

The movement of money indicates the movement of the heart. Where money goes, the heart goes also. A relationship exists between money and the heart, and that is why it's so important for us to guard our hearts.

Money, whether it's a significant or small amount, has a unique, and possibly even an innate, ability to pressure the human heart into submission and make itself a tyrant in our lives. This is why it is significant that we embrace the biblical truths within this story and put money in its proper place.

We must work diligently to maintain a biblically centered perspective on our finances.

Money is a tool to be used for good, helping us sustain our lives, provide for our families, support the church's mission, and assist those in need. It is not the target for which we aim our lives. Hitting this target is actually tragic.

Money is a tool, not the target.

> What good is it for someone to gain the whole world,
> yet forfeit their soul?
> **MARK 8:36**

It's also important for us to strive to establish biblically centered priorities when it comes to where we spend or place our money. How do we do this?

> But seek first his kingdom and his righteousness,
> and all these things will be given to you as well.
> **MATTHEW 6:33**

"Seek first the kingdom of God," as Jesus says in Matthew. Then we turn to God in prayer and ask Him to help us determine our remaining financial priorities.

We must establish and maintain biblically centered practices for how we earn our money. The world watches what we Christians do at work. Let's show them we don't live by utilitarian mantras like, "Make as much as you can by any means necessary."

Instead, let's prove to them that we live by the words of Micah 6:8.

> And what does the LORD require of you? To act justly
> and to love mercy and to walk humbly with your God.
> **MICAH 6:8**

And finally, it's imperative that we keep one tree in mind at all times: the tree on which Jesus died. It's important to remember how that tree represents our freedom from the tyranny of sin, guilt, and greed.

By giving our lives to *the Life of the Party*, the One who died for us, we acknowledge one God, one Lord, one Ruler, one Heart's Keeper, and one Treasure's Master. When we make Jesus the center of our lives, we will be given the strength we need to put money in its proper place.

We will be empowered by Him to boldly proclaim the words below from Joshua.

Choose for yourselves this day whom you will serve ...
But as for me and my household, we will serve the LORD.
JOSHUA 24:15B

 **THOUGHT-PROVOKING PARTY FOOD**

1. How does our culture view money?

2. How easily can it become a dominant force in our lives?

3. Why do you think Zacchaeus was so affected by Jesus? What was it about Jesus that impacted the change in Zacchaeus' way of thinking?

4. How do we ensure material wealth doesn't become excessive?

5. What's the difference between ownership and stewardship?

Six days before the Passover, Jesus came to Bethany, where Lazarus lived, whom Jesus had raised from the dead. Here, a dinner was given in Jesus' honor. Martha served while Lazarus was among those reclining at the table with him. Then Mary took about a pint of pure nard, an expensive perfume; she poured it on Jesus' feet and wiped his feet with her hair. And the house was filled with the fragrance of the perfume.

But one of his disciples, Judas Iscariot, who was later to betray him, objected, "Why wasn't this perfume sold and the money given to the poor? It was worth a year's wages."

He did not say this because he cared about the poor but because he was a thief; as keeper of the money bag, he used to help himself to what was put into it.

"Leave her alone," Jesus replied. "It was intended that she should save this perfume for the day of my burial. You will always have the poor among you, but you will not always have me."

Meanwhile, a large crowd of Jews found out that Jesus was there and came, not only because of him but also to see Lazarus, whom he had raised from the dead.

JOHN 12:1-9

—CHAPTER 9—
Dinner Party

GOLF IS A DIFFICULT and challenging sport. It's unbelievable how much trouble this small ball can cause. It's hard to believe that we make such a big deal over something so little. The impact a golf ball has on fully grown adults is hard to fathom.

Think about the power that a gold ball has: This little ball can make people jump up and down with joy. It can prompt people to interact with it regularly, and it can even entice people into kissing it. It can bring out the best in people, and it can also bring out the worst.

This little ball can bring grown men to tears. And it has the power to control the tongue. Did you know that someone conducted a study on the effects of cussing on golf? For such a refined sport, often associated with gentle people, it was found that swearing was considered a "relief valve" that many golfers need when playing under pressure!

When I was in high school, I knew a youth pastor, Pastor Steve, who loved to golf—even though he wasn't very good at it. I played with him several times and never saw him get mad. Steve never lost his temper. He was always having fun and always cool, calm, and collected.

In fact, whenever he hit a bad shot off the tee, which was often, he would actually smile and shout, "Glory Hallelujah!"

Steve would hit one in the water and yell, "Praise the Lord!" He wasn't doing this to be funny, and he wasn't substituting these phrases for the classic phrases some golfers use after a bad shot.

Steve was genuine; he was authentic. And his authenticity was not dependent upon where he was in the moment or what he was doing.

Pastor Steve loved Jesus. He loved to talk about Jesus and praise Him. When it came to living for Jesus, people said Steve was dramatic, excessive, and over-the-top, which was exactly what people said about Mary, the sister of Martha and Lazarus.

GUESS WHO'S COMING TO DINNER?

In John 11, Mary and her sister Martha were busy preparing the body of their brother, Lazarus, for burial. However, in the scripture reference we just read in Chapter 12, both of them are now hosting an event in their home in Jesus' honor. They are busily preparing dinner because they know *the Life of the Party* is on His way.

Hosting a nice dinner was the least they could do for Jesus, considering He had just raised their brother from the dead a few weeks earlier. When He walked up to the tomb, He told the bystanders, "Take away the stone," and with the voice that rebuked demons and calmed the storm, yelled, "Lazarus, come forth."

For Mary and Martha, preparing a homemade meal for Jesus, the One who spoke life into their brother's decaying, bound, and bandaged body, is a sign of their appreciation and an act of gratitude.

Now, let's take a moment to think about this dinner.

For the fun of it, let's quickly run through the guest list here and name the people who are dining in Bethany, who are now reclining around the table. The guest list for this dinner party is unlike any other guest list in history. That's for sure! There are some very historically significant and famous people.

First of all, Jesus—*the Life of the Party* and the Son of God—is in the room, which is a pretty big deal, don't you think?

Since the Passover is less than a week away, all the disciples are there, too. So we're talking about Peter, James, and John—some of the most influential people in history. They're lounging around the table as well.

Of course, Judas is also present, and unfortunately, he's also famous (clearly for different reasons). Apparently, he's there to offer a skeptical commentary on the evening's events and to serve as the critic in the room. Hey! Every party has a party pooper, and Judas is it on this night.

Who else is at this dinner party?

Mary and Martha are obviously in the house. After all, they're the ones hosting this little get-together. They're the hospitality team, so to speak. But they're not just there as hosts. They're also at this meal because, even though they're not considered part of the twelve, they're some of Jesus' disciples too. Jesus' response to Mary in this story validates the fact that she is just as much a disciple as any of the men in the room.

So this is quite a group of people who have gathered for dinner, wouldn't you agree?

Let's see, though. Someone is still missing from our guest list. Someone whose presence is sort of, kind of, a big deal in this story. Who else of importance have I yet to mention? Lazarus!

Hello! We can't forget to mention Lazarus. His presence at this dinner party is pretty powerful. I mean, after all, if there's anyone in this room who has firsthand knowledge of the life and love Jesus offers, it's him. It's Lazarus. His story is incredible.

The fact that Lazarus is now actually reclining around the table, rather than lying in his grave, is monumentally amazing. It's not an everyday occurrence—people getting to dine with a man who has been raised from the dead—which makes this dining experience unlike any other, to say the least.

Now, can you picture this scene? Can you visualize all these different people gathered and reclining in Lazarus's home? And can you imagine the conversations they might be having around the table?

"Hey, Andrew, isn't this fish we're eating tonight the same kind of fish Jesus used to feed the five thousand?"

And Peter says, "Wow! You have got to taste the wine! It's so good—almost as good as the stuff Jesus made at that wedding in Cana. Uh, Jesus, there's a pot of water right over there, so what do you think? How about you do your thing and keep this party going?"

I can definitely imagine someone in the room looking over at Lazarus and saying, "So Lazarus, how's life treatin' you these days?" Can you picture this?

I'm sure the conversation around this table was fascinating. It always is when Jesus is present, and I bet the food was terrific.

I imagine that Mary and Martha prepared the meal of a lifetime for Jesus. Wouldn't you if He came over for dinner at your house? I mean, if I knew Jesus was coming to my house for dinner, I don't think I would order in pizza. No. The food at this dinner party was probably something very special, and the conversation was perhaps lively.

THE REAL HOST WITH THE MOST

However, the highlight of this evening has nothing to do with food or drink, and the centerpiece of this story is unrelated to the various conversations the guests may or may not be having around the table.

The highlight of this evening is Mary's response to the overwhelming love Jesus has shown her family.

Sometime during the meal, while Martha is serving dinner, something begins to move deep within Mary's heart. She's already demonstrating a deep sense of gratitude for what Jesus has done for her and her family by hosting this dinner.

This dinner is a generous and hospitable gesture of thanksgiving, but in Mary's mind, it's just not enough.

Mary feels compelled to do more. Her soul longs to do more, but she doesn't know what to do—yet.

I imagine that at some point during dinner, Mary looks across the room at Lazarus in amazement. There he is, her brother, alive and well.

He's never looked so good, never seemed so alive.

Because the power and love of Jesus came upon him, he's now radiating with life. The brother Mary had buried and placed in a cold, dark, despair-filled tomb is now reclining at her dinner table. He's laughing, smiling, and retelling the story about how just the sound of Jesus' voice alone brought him back to life!

As Mary's eyes and thoughts slowly shift away from Lazarus, they eventually land on Jesus. Now I wonder what is going through her mind when she looks at Jesus.

One look at Jesus reminds her of the day her brother died.

One look at Jesus reminds her of her sorrow, her tears, her heartache, her feelings of hopelessness, and her inability to even breathe because the pain was so great.

One look at Jesus reminds her of his humanity, reminds her that Jesus cried too, and how they cried together as He comforted her in a way that only Jesus can.

But one look at Jesus also reminds Mary of the unthinkable, the unimaginable, the miraculous moment she witnessed with her very own eyes. The moment Jesus turned her sorrow into joy. The moment Jesus proved He had authority over death was when He raised her brother from the dead.

One look at Jesus is all it takes to bring Jesus' words back to her mind. As if it were yesterday, she can still hear Jesus saying, "I am the Resurrection and the Life. He who believes in Me will live, even though he dies, and whoever lives and believes in Me will never die."

Seeing Jesus reminds Mary of His supernatural power and His unstoppable love!

Mary looks over at Jesus, and this causes her to come undone; she's completely overrun and overwhelmed by His love. And she needs to, she must, she has to respond somehow, in some way.

Mary has to respond to the love of Christ.

I don't believe she knows how to respond at first; I really don't. I don't think she planned what she's about to do beforehand. Her response in this story seems spontaneous; it appears driven by love rather than reason.

So, with love leading the way, Mary quickly searches throughout the house in haste for something of value, something of worth, something of importance—a precious gift, a treasured offering, a prized possession—to give to Jesus as a sign of her love and a symbol of her highest praise.

Her love leads her to a pint of costly perfume, equivalent to the annual income of one person.

Mary probably doesn't realize that God is working within her at this moment, using her to prepare another body for burial. Jesus' body. Mary doesn't recognize the future significance of her present offering. Later on, I'm sure she does, but in this moment, she doesn't. She is simply responding to Jesus' love in her own way.

So she takes this pint of perfume and responds to His love.

First, Mary responds with humility. In this ancient context, it's considered to be a high honor to anoint someone's head with oil. Mary considers herself unworthy of such an honor, so she decides to humbly anoint Jesus' feet.

Mary responds to Jesus' love with boldness. It was unacceptable for a woman at this time to ever let her hair down in public. No respectable woman would ever do what Mary is about to do. Still, Mary doesn't care what is or isn't acceptable in the eyes of society when it comes to glorifying the

Son of God. She doesn't care if she loses respect over her act of adoration. Mary wants to ensure that Jesus receives the respect He deserves.

And Mary responds to Jesus' love with extravagance.

Most people in this situation would only use a drop or two when anointing someone, but Mary anoints Jesus with a pint of perfume—the whole pound. She pours the entire sixteen ounces on Jesus' feet.

It's strong enough to fill the entire house with its fragrance, like a Febreze air freshener. It's strong enough to make everybody else's clothes smell fresh and sweet. It's strong enough to stay on Jesus' feet as He walks His cross down the Via Dolorosa one week later!

Now talk about excessive!

Talk about being dramatic and over-the-top. Mary's characteristics stem from her complete response of love and resources to Christ.

The love of God in Christ moves Mary to action and to adoration. It moves her to worship.

This same love that Mary experiences in the depths of her soul, this same love that compels her to pour her perfume on Jesus, this same love that causes her to wash His feet with her tears and dry them with her hair, is the same love that moves us to adoration and action. It's the same love that moves us to worship the One who loves us so much.

We are moved to worship Jesus because of who He is. He's *the Life of the Party*—the Son of God.

We are also moved to worship Jesus because of what He has done for us on the cross. Jesus emptied out His life for you and for me. More precious than any fragrance in the universe, Jesus poured out His blood. He laid down His life for all humanity and continues to pour out His love on all those who accept Him as their Savior and their Lord.

When it comes to pouring out love, Jesus is as dramatic, excessive, and over-the-top as you can get.

We are moved to worship Christ because each one of us is a modern-day Lazarus.

God's love and power in Jesus Christ have raised us from death to life, from despair to hope, from bondage to freedom, and from the tomb to the table.

Now we can recline with Jesus and talk with Him anywhere, at any time, through the power of the Holy Spirit.

We are moved to worship Christ because each of us is a modern-day Mary. We have looked into the face of Christ, and just one glance reminds us of His supernatural power and His unending love.

Just one look at Jesus reminds us that He alone is worthy of our worship, and that we should worship Him with humility, boldness, and extravagance, just as Mary did.

Just one look at our Savior compels us to look around our lives for something of value, something of worth, something of importance. A precious gift, a treasured offering, a prized possession—to offer up as *our* highest gift of praise. Our highest gift of thanksgiving.

Just one look at Jesus moves us to pour out our praise on him, which is why we gather at churches every week. At these gatherings, some of us are often moved to raise our hands in praise, while others sit quietly in awe and wonder at God's grace and goodness. Some of us are compelled to shout for joy now and then; one or two of us are even motivated to clap our hands.

We are moved by the Spirit to do these things in worship. Why?

Because Jesus—*the Life of the Party*—is worthy of our worship! And because Jesus just keeps pouring out His love on all those who call out to Him, we are driven—we are compelled, we want, we long to do more for Jesus, to show Him our gratitude. And we can do more.

Each one of us in Christ is not only a modern-day Lazarus who has been raised with Christ, and not only a modern-day Mary being led by love to respond to love, but also the perfume in this passage.

Our lives are the precious offerings. The greatest gift we can give Jesus is the gift of ourselves. When we pour ourselves out completely at the feet of Jesus as we worship, a fragrance of praise, unlike any other, permeates our world. And Jesus is honored, respected, and glorified.

But as Mary shows us in our story today, worship isn't just about adoration. It's about action as well. Mary didn't just say, "Jesus, you are worthy of my worship." She didn't just shout, "Glory Hallelujah! Praise the Lord!"

Mary showed Jesus and others just how worthy of worship He really is by pouring her perfume and her praise on Him.

Worship involves adoration and action, which means our worship doesn't end after the benediction. It doesn't end when we leave church on Sunday.

Actually, our worship begins there. Because after we pour ourselves out at the feet of Jesus in a church service, we must pour ourselves out at the feet of Jesus in the world.

And we pour ourselves out at the feet of Jesus by pouring our lives out for others: for those in need, for those in pain, for the hurting and the sick, for the imprisoned, and the neglected, for the forsaken and forgotten, for our families, for our friends, and for our children.

So yes, we worship in a service. Then, in service, we worship. Our worship ought to smell really good in church. It ought to smell really good in the world.

When it comes to our worship, when it comes to pouring our lives out for God in church, when it comes to pouring our lives out for others in the world, and when it comes to pouring our love of God in Christ on people, I hope people look at us and say we're dramatic, a little excessive, and way over the top. I hope people see *the Life of the Party* working in and through us.

Therefore, I urge you, brothers and sisters, in view of God's mercy, to offer your bodies as a living sacrifice, holy and pleasing to God—this is your true and proper worship.
ROMANS 12:1

THOUGHT-PROVOKING PARTY FOOD

1. Of all the characters in this story, who do you see yourself in the most?

2. Consider our lives as a poured-out offering—what are your thoughts?

3. How is this story connected to Romans 12:1?

4. How does this narrative affect our understanding of worship?

5. What has Jesus recently done to inspire your actions for Him?

On the evening of that first day of the week, when the disciples were together, with the doors locked for fear of the Jewish leaders, Jesus came and stood among them and said, "Peace be with you!" After he said this, he showed them his hands and side. The disciples were overjoyed when they saw the Lord.

Again Jesus said, "Peace be with you! As the Father has sent me, I am sending you." And with that he breathed on them and said, "Receive the Holy Spirit. If you forgive anyone's sins, their sins are forgiven; if you do not forgive them, they are not forgiven."

Now Thomas (also known as Didymus), one of the Twelve, was not with the disciples when Jesus came. So the other disciples told him, "We have seen the Lord!"

But he said to them, "Unless I see the nail marks in his hands and put my finger where the nails were, and put my hand into his side, I will not believe."

A week later his disciples were in the house again, and Thomas was with them. Though the doors were locked, Jesus came and stood among them and said, "Peace be with you!" Then he said to Thomas, "Put your finger here; see my hands. Reach out your hand and put it into my side. Stop doubting and believe."

Thomas said to him, "My Lord and my God!"

Then Jesus told him, "Because you have seen me, you have believed; blessed are those who have not seen and yet have believed."

Jesus performed many other signs in the presence of his disciples, which are not recorded in this book. But these are written that you may believe that Jesus is the Messiah, the Son of God, and that by believing you may have life in his name.

JOHN 20:19-31

—CHAPTER 10—
Surprise Party

I LOVE SURPRISE PARTIES. They're a lot of fun, especially when you're with the group doing the surprising!

There's so much excitement in the air right before the person you're going to surprise walks through the door, which is when the fun begins.

The lookout yells, "Get into place! They're here!" Everyone scatters and scrambles to find that perfect hiding place behind a counter or a couch. Then the keeper of the lights turns them out, and the shushing begins.

In those few moments right before the door opens and the guest of honor comes in through the door, you can really feel the energy in the room.

Everybody has their party favors in hand and is poised, ready to yell out, "Surprise!" as soon as he or she walks in the room. And then, after the surprise, you gotta love the expression on his or her face. Priceless.

Surprise parties are great, especially the one in this story. What we have here is the greatest surprise party in history: the moment Jesus, *the Life of the Party*, suddenly appears to His friends and surprises them.

But this isn't your typical surprise party. This isn't at all how surprise parties work, is it?

In fact, what we see in this passage is the opposite of what we think of when we think of a surprise party. Instead of having a group of people surprise one person, we have one person surprising the whole group. Instead of having a group of people full of energy and anxiously anticipating the joy they're about to give to another, *they're* the ones who are about to experience the joy and energy that another is going to bring into the room unannounced. The anticipated joy of giving is replaced by the unexpected joy of receiving, a gift that mirrors Jesus' entrance.

He surprises his disciples, and I'm sure that they're not just surprised but shocked.

I can't imagine a better surprise party than the one the disciples experience in this passage. Wouldn't you love to have seen the expressions on the faces of the disciples the moment Jesus suddenly appeared?

What the disciples experience is a huge surprise, and because of this, John tells us that they rejoice and celebrate. This is a surprise party unlike any other.

Picture the scene. Here are the disciples, all gathered on Sunday evening in someone's house with the doors locked. *Heavily* locked with a large bolt slid through rings attached to the door and its frame.

And why are the doors locked? Because they're scared to death. They're thinking that the Jewish authorities might want to crucify them too, since they're followers of Jesus.

Now, you wouldn't think they would be scared because this isn't just any given Sunday. It is Resurrection Sunday, the day Jesus is raised from the dead. They've all heard the news. Peter and John told them the grave is empty. Mary told them that she had actually seen Jesus.

But they're still frightened by the night and uncertain about their futures.

Maybe John isn't. Maybe by now, Peter isn't either, but most of them are afraid. And in this state of paralyzing fear and overwhelming anxiety, surprise! Jesus appears with all the power of the Resurrection and all the joy of the Lord.

So here's Jesus, suddenly standing in their presence, amid their fear and anxiety, and what are the first words He speaks to them? "Peace be with you." He says, "Peace!" or "Shalom!"

Of course, we could say that He's simply using the common Jewish greeting of the day. Or that He's using the standard first-liner that angels use in the Bible when they begin talking, so people aren't overwhelmed with shock. However, I believe Jesus' words are intentional.

JESUS WILL ALWAYS SHOW UP

His first words to them reveal a great deal about who Jesus is and what you receive when He enters your life, your context, and your situation.

Whenever and wherever Jesus shows up, He always brings the peace of God with Him, through the power of the Holy Spirit. Whether in bodily form in a room full of disciples on the day of His Resurrection, or in a church worship service, He's ready to give His peace to anyone who asks for it. No matter the place. No matter the time of day.

In this story, Jesus appears, amid the disciples' fear and anxiety, as the Prince of Peace. Then Jesus shows them His hands and side, so they can now know that He's the same Jesus who died on the cross.

He isn't a ghost, an impersonator, or a resuscitated man who didn't really die, as some critics claim.

No, He is the same Jesus who is now alive and vibrant, filled with the power of the Resurrection.

And because He's filled with the power of the Resurrection, His body's no longer bound by the laws of nature. He now moves freely between the physical and spiritual worlds.

Jesus stands before them with a resurrected body, and, after a second greeting of peace, says two more interesting things.

First, He says, "As the Father has sent me, so I send you." Jesus is giving them their new life mission: to go and tell others about Him and His love!

Secondly, Jesus promises them the Holy Spirit.

They don't receive the Holy Spirit here, just the promise that they'll receive the Holy Spirit. We know this because the Greek verb here specifically tells us that Jesus breathed *on/onto* the disciples and not *into* them. We also know from Acts that the Holy Spirit doesn't come into them until fifty days later at Pentecost.

At Pentecost, they are filled with the Holy Spirit; the Spirit is not just *on* them, but *within* them.

So Jesus gives the disciples three things here: peace, purpose, and a promise. Wow! They had to be so energized.

However, not all the disciples are there to see Jesus and receive His peace, His mission for them, and His promise of the Holy Spirit. Who's missing? Thomas and Judas.

We know what happened to Judas, right? Not good.

But where is Thomas?

Why is he not with the other disciples? What was he doing? Did he step out for some fresh air? Did he draw the short straw and have to go out for some firewood or some fresh goat's milk?

We don't know what he was doing, but what a missed opportunity! Jesus appears to the disciples, alive as can be, and Thomas misses it. Thomas gets back to the house, from wherever he had been, and is likely to wonder what all the hype is about.

They tell him that Jesus is alive and that they saw Him. But Thomas doesn't believe them.

He's a skeptic. He wants proof. He wants empirical data. He wants to see the mark of the nails in Jesus' hands and put his finger in those marks. And he wants to put his hand on the side of Jesus, where He was pierced.

He will not believe until he gets the proof he's looking for. And this is why Thomas gets a bad rap. It is the reason he earns the name "Doubting Thomas."

So he doubts? So what? What's wrong with that? What's wrong with having doubts?

Nothing. It's normal. At one time or another in our lives, each one of us is like Doubting Thomas. Sometimes we lack faith and want some real, tangible, empirical proof to strengthen our faith.

There are times when we wish we could put our hands on Jesus' side and our fingers in the nail marks on His hands to see if He's for real.

Unfortunately, we can't do that—not yet, at least. But we can receive validation for our faith.

We might not be able to touch Jesus' hands and side, but we are invited to *taste and see that the Lord is good*, as David says in Psalm 34.

> Taste and see that the LORD is good;
> blessed is the one who takes refuge in him.
> **PSALM 34:8**

And we are promised that when we search for God, we will find Him, when we search for Him with all our hearts.

> You will seek me and find me
> when you seek me with all your heart.
> **JEREMIAH 29:13**

So, if we ever doubt, like Thomas did, and are skeptics, then the way to overcome our doubts and skepticism is to continue searching for all that God is doing and to keep walking by faith. God will provide the validation and assurance we are looking for when we look to Him.

Thomas needs some assurance, and Jesus knows this, so He gives him exactly what he needs.

One week later, the disciples were in the room again with the door shut, but this time, it was not locked.

That's interesting. They may be feeling a little more confident now, knowing that Jesus is alive. This time, Thomas is with them when they get surprised. Jesus suddenly shows up and offers His peace again.

But this time, He looks right at Thomas and invites him to see and feel the mark of the nails. Then Jesus says, "Do not doubt, but believe!" Immediately, Thomas believes and says, "My Lord and my God!"

Thomas becomes the first person to recognize Jesus as the Son of God.

Now, Thomas has brought us full circle regarding who Jesus is, as per the Gospel of John.

In the beginning was the Word, and the Word was with God, and the Word was God. He was with God in the beginning. Through him all things were made; without him nothing was made that has been made. In him was life, and that life was the light of all mankind. The light shines in the darkness, and the darkness has not overcome it.

JOHN 1:1-5

John begins his Gospel by telling us, "In the beginning was the Word (Jesus), and the Word was with God, and the Word was God." He tells us about the incarnation, in which God becomes human. Additionally, he shares with us information about Jesus' ministry, His messages, His crucifixion and death, and His Resurrection.

And now, John gives us the story of Thomas' encounter with Jesus to remind us who Jesus is.

He's *the Life of the Party.*

Jesus is God wrapped in human flesh. He took on our sin and conquered death. He was raised from the dead and is the giver of life.

At this moment, Thomas believes. He has faith. Thomas has faith in the resurrected Christ, which means he trusts Jesus as his Lord and his God. He believes Jesus reigns in his life.

Thomas's faith is life-giving, just like John says in verse 31: "Anyone who believes in Jesus has life in His name."

Thomas' faith moves him to action.

His faith in Jesus is a belief in action. Tradition suggests that Thomas carried Jesus' love and message to the East. We know he went east, and some say that he made it all the way to India. The man's faith in Jesus changed the course of his life. He lived wholeheartedly for Jesus and died as a martyr for Him.

This is the *real* Thomas. And that is how we should remember him.

Many people today still refer to him as "Doubting Thomas." But that's not true! He is "Believing Thomas," who has also become:

- Obedient to his Lord and God, Thomas.
- Faith-filled and faithful, Thomas.
- Full-of-life, Thomas.
- On fire for the gospel, Thomas.
- Hardworking, people-loving, Thomas.
- Bold and courageous, Thomas.
- Willing to do whatever it takes to tell others about Jesus, Thomas.
- Go wherever he needs to go, Thomas.

I like the new Thomas and would like to be him. Wouldn't you? I'd like us all to be like new Thomas.

Let us strive to serve Jesus with the same faithfulness that Thomas showed. I pray God makes us people who will do whatever we need to do to pursue God. And that He will strengthen our faith so that we will be people of faith who bring the peace of Christ wherever we go.

Also, I pray our faith, like Thomas', will inspire us to action. When people see our hands serving, I pray they see Jesus' hand at work.

And I pray that whatever level of faith we might have, we will have countless chances to *surprise* people with the love of Jesus, *the Life of the Party*.

 **THOUGHT-PROVOKING PARTY FOOD**

1. When was the last time you felt the peace of God in your life?

2. What are some ways God has surprised you?

3. What is the influence of doubt on our lives?

4. When does faith lead to action?

5. What are some ways that you can trust God today?

A few days later, when Jesus again entered Capernaum, the people heard that he had come home. They gathered in such large numbers that there was no room left, not even outside the door, and he preached the word to them. Some men came, bringing to him a paralyzed man, carried by four of them. Since they could not get him to Jesus because of the crowd, they made an opening in the roof above Jesus by digging through it and then lowered the mat the man was lying on. When Jesus saw their faith, he said to the paralyzed man, "Son, your sins are forgiven."

Now some teachers of the law were sitting there, thinking to themselves, "Why does this fellow talk like that? He's blaspheming! Who can forgive sins but God alone?"

Immediately Jesus knew in his spirit that this was what they were thinking in their hearts, and he said to them, "Why are you thinking these things? Which is easier: to say to this paralyzed man, 'Your sins are forgiven,' or to say, 'Get up, take your mat and walk'? But I want you to know that the Son of Man has authority on earth to forgive sins." So he said to the man, "I tell you, get up, take your mat and go home." He got up, took his mat and walked out in full view of them all.

This amazed everyone and they praised God, saying, "We have never seen anything like this!"

MARK 2:1-12

—CHAPTER 11—
Dance Party

I LOVE THIS STORY, taken from the book of Mark. It's a good one and one of my favorites. Of course, any story featuring Jesus is a good one.

When I read this story, I am catapulted back to my childhood. Closing my eyes, a picture forms of myself as a kid in Sunday school at my small country church. While listening to my Sunday school teacher talk about this story, I am coloring the lesson page she handed out. I used to love coloring. Those were the days. You know you had it good when the toughest decision of your day was trying to figure out what color crayon to use. I loved coloring and learning about Jesus. About 90% of the Bible verses and stories I know were learned and memorized during my childhood Sunday school years.

That's why I'm such a big fan of children and youth ministries. Immersing our children in God's Word is essential. Also, it's essential to continue coloring! It can be a spiritual practice. I'm not sure why some of us stop coloring when we become adults.

When reading this story, there's an odd thing that happens. Lionel Richie pops into my head while reading Mark 2:12. I like Lionel Richie's music, and seeing him in concert a few years ago, when he came to The Woodlands, was a great experience!

It's quite possible I was one of the youngest people there.

Usually, I get teased because I like his music, but that's okay. It doesn't bother me; it rolls right off my back. I'm not phased at all because, as the song goes, *I'm easy like Sunday morning.*

Right now, you must be thinking, *Jason, why in the world would Lionel Richie come to your mind when you read this passage?* Because when reading it, Lionel Richie's song "Dancing on the Ceiling" plays in my mind.

Think about it. Four men carry their friend on top of a house, tear a hole in the roof, then lower their friend down to Jesus. Jesus heals this man while the others look down through the hole they have just cut. After Jesus heals this man, everyone (Mark says) praises God. Everyone includes these guys.

If I were one of these guys and just saw my friend healed, I know I'd be dancing on the ceiling. These friends would be too.

Now do you see why I think of Lionel when I read this passage? I hope you do!

This story has a great ending, but it also has a great beginning. At the beginning of this passage, the people in the area already know that if you find Jesus, you'll find a celebration. You'll find a party! Locate Jesus and you'll find unspeakable joy and fullness of life! Hang around Jesus long enough and you'll be in for a treat: something powerful, something good will happen.

Chances are you'll witness a miracle. You'll see somebody get healed. Witnessing those miracles explains why Jesus' popularity is off the charts!

Mark concludes Chapter 1 with the news that Jesus and his miracles were spreading like wildfire. Jesus couldn't even enter a town without getting swarmed by the masses. He was a magnet! Look at the last verse of Mark, Chapter 1.

Instead he went out and began to talk freely, spreading the news.
As a result, Jesus could no longer enter a town openly
but stayed outside in lonely places.
Yet the people still came to him from everywhere.
MARK 1:45

Here, Mark states, "people still came to him from everywhere!" When Jesus returns to Capernaum in Chapter 2, the hype surrounding Jesus is crazy-insane. This made Capernaum a city full of energy and activity. Capernaum is alive like New York City on New Year's Eve. Why? Because Jesus is there!

THE NEW YORK CITY OF BIBLICAL TIMES

Now, let's take a quick look at four significant and interesting aspects of Capernaum, as it was a significant town to Jesus.

1. In Jesus' time, Capernaum was a fishing village on the Northern end of the Sea of Galilee; this was Peter's hometown. Peter was a fisherman by trade until Jesus called him and transformed him into a fisher of people.
2. The name Capernaum means "Nahum's Village." Nahum was a prophet in the Old Testament. The name Nahum means "Comforter," which makes Capernaum the "Village of the Comforter." How perfect is that? Jesus, who can offer and give comfort like no one else, chose to reside in the Village of the Comforter.
3. Capernaum was built alongside a major ancient road called the "Via Maris." The Via Maris led from Damascus to Tiberius and then down to Egypt. You talk about being strategic. Jesus chose to reside in a town next to one of the busiest ancient trade routes, facilitating travel and communication between Asia and Africa. Jesus positioned himself to spread his message of love and life rapidly between Asia and Africa.
4. Finally, many people in ancient times traveled down Via Maris from the north and stopped at Capernaum on their way to Tiberius (much like Buc-ee's for people heading to Dallas). In ancient times, people traveled through Capernaum down to Tiberius because it had many natural hot springs. Tiberius was like an ancient day spa with hot tubs from that era.

But people didn't go there to relax. They believed that these hot springs in Tiberius could bring healing.

Many people would travel through Capernaum, down to Tiberias, hoping that somehow, someway, they could experience the miraculous. Of course, these hot springs weren't magical. Maybe they were good for the skin, but they couldn't cure diseases. They couldn't make the lame walk, or the blind see, or the deaf hear, or cure leprosy. Bathing in these hot waters was just pointless. It was an exercise in futility—the equivalent of throwing a coin into a wishing well.

But when Jesus arrives and begins His ministry, the hot spot is no longer Tiberius. It's Capernaum because Jesus is there—Jesus, the One who is the source of healing. Somehow, someway, four men hear Jesus is in Capernaum and know they must take their friend to Him.

What do we know about these men? Not much, just that they are four guys who want to help their friend. We don't know how or when these guys heard about Jesus and that He was in Capernaum, but we can speculate. Maybe they were on their way to Tiberius with their friend when they first heard the buzz about Jesus. Maybe, when heading to the hot springs on Via Maris, they changed course after meeting someone who said real healing was in Capernaum. Or maybe these guys just got back from Tiberius.

They could have dunked their paralyzed friend in the hot springs and deemed it a complete waste of time. Then, after they heard about the Miracle Worker, they hurried back to Capernaum. Perhaps they'd previously failed miserably at Tiberius with their friend.

It's possible that there were many times before, when people hoped the hot springs in Tiberius could work miracles. Did they see the Capernaum crowds upon their return and join the throng to see Jesus?

Even though it's likely that these men went to Tiberius with their friend at some point, the truth remains that we know little about these guys. We don't know where they're from, how much they had tried to help their friend before this day began, or how they heard about Jesus.

However, we know this: they were serious, very serious, about doing whatever it took to get their friend to Jesus. They would not wait for the crowd to die out. Neither would they be looking at the sun or a sundial and think they were running out of daylight. There was no thought of going back tomorrow, and that tomorrow is the perfect day for everything, anyway. These guys would not pick a number and wait in line.

Considering the situation, no thought was given to how big or chaotic the crowd was, or that after pushing through it, there would be no room for them.

No! These guys would not be stopped or deterred by the crowds.

They believed they must and could get their friend to Jesus. It would require hard work, more time than they had planned, and thinking outside the box. Well, they are that. These guys were tenacious and persistent, out-of-the-box thinkers.

Can you imagine the conversation they had right before they climbed up on the house?

Imagine one guy saying, *Listen, guys! You know I love our buddy here, but I'm done dragging him ten miles all the way down to Tiberius to fail. Let's try this Jesus. I believe he's the real deal. Let's make it happen, and let's do it now!*

The homes in this region were built into hills, so imagine one of the other three guys saying, *Yeah, let's go for it! We can do it. Jesus is in that house. The four of us can carry our friend up the hill, cut a hole in the roof, and lower him down to Jesus. Who cares if we ruin the roof? Whatever it takes to get to Jesus, right? The roof can always be replaced.*

What a scene this must have been! Can you picture these guys cutting a hole in the roof? Can you imagine the pieces of the roof, made of dried mud and reeds, falling onto Jesus and getting in His hair?

Can you picture the expression on Jesus' face as He looks up and sees this man being lowered into His presence? Jesus had to smile, don't you think? Or at least a smirk, right?

And then, imagine hearing Jesus speak with such a commanding presence. Can you imagine being in the room, or on top of the roof, when Jesus says two life-changing, life-altering phrases? "Son, your sins are forgiven." And "Get up, take your mat and go home."

A paralyzed man, in desperation, was lowered through a hole in a roof, got up, and walked out the front door. It must have been a sight to see.

No wonder everybody was praising God! They were dancing on the ceiling, saying, "We've never seen anything like this!"

Of course, they had seen nothing like this because they had never seen anyone like Jesus! He's one of a kind; there is none like Him!

This man had to be walking, not just around the house, but also on cloud nine. Because not only was his body healed, but he was also set free from his sins. Those are two important reasons he should praise God!

This man had a lot to be thankful for, didn't he? I hope Jesus was the first person he thanked. Jesus turned this man's life around. Jesus, the source of living water, gave this man something that no water in any hot spring could ever give him.

Having thanked Jesus, I hope he got to the roof and thanked his friends. Because when it came to friendship, these four guys were amazing!

Think about it.

- They heard the buzz and believed.
- They heard about Jesus, *the Life of the Party*, had faith in His power and ability to heal, and then acted on that faith.
- They were all in, pulling out all the stops, and going above and beyond.

- They jumped in with both feet and dove in headfirst!
- They seized the day! *Carpe diem*!

No matter the metaphor, these men were tenacious, creative, persistent, and bold, doing whatever it took to introduce their friend to Jesus. Now that's what you call faith. That's what you call friendship.

Here are some ideas to consider:

- What if we, the church today, Christians around the world, became more like these four friends?
- What if we read the Bible like never before and allowed ourselves to get caught up in the buzz about Jesus?
- What if we believed the same Jesus in the Bible, who was in Capernaum, is everywhere through the power of the Holy Spirit?
- What if we believed He's within everyone who follows Him?
- Imagine, like those friends, what might follow if we acted on our faith in Jesus.
- What would happen if we were just as tenacious, persistent, bold, and creative as they were in bringing people to Jesus?

Indeed, people are surrounding us who urgently require knowledge of the unconditional love, hope, grace, truth, and healing available through Jesus.

In doing everything we can to introduce them to Jesus, what if we pulled out all the stops, went all in, above and beyond, jumped in with both feet, dove in headfirst, and seized the day?

I'll tell you what would happen. More people would come to Christ and come to know what it's like to hear Jesus say, "Son/daughter, your sins are forgiven." They would come to know what it's like to be set free from sin, guilt, and shame.

If we were more like these friends, these out-of-the-box thinkers, willing to climb on top of houses and metaphorically cut holes in roofs, heaven would be packed.

There would be crowds of people ready to worship God, eager to encounter our Savior, Jesus Christ. Not just *the Life of the Party*, but also The Way, the Truth, and the Life!

 **THOUGHT-PROVOKING PARTY FOOD**

1. Define friendship.

2. The friends in this story were amazingly devoted and creative when it came to helping their friend in need. Have you ever seen friendship like this before? If so, what was it like?

3. Describe a time in your life when you felt like dancing!

When Jesus had again crossed over by boat to the other side of the lake, a large crowd gathered around him while he was by the lake. Then one of the synagogue leaders, named Jairus, came, and when he saw Jesus, he fell at his feet. He pleaded earnestly with him, "My little daughter is dying. Please come and put your hands on her so that she will be healed and live." So Jesus went with him.

A large crowd followed and pressed around him. And a woman was there who had been subject to bleeding for twelve years. She had suffered a great deal under the care of many doctors and had spent all she had, yet instead of getting better she grew worse. When she heard about Jesus, she came up behind him in the crowd and touched his cloak, because she thought, "If I just touch his clothes, I will be healed." Immediately her bleeding stopped and she felt in her body that she was freed from her suffering.

At once Jesus realized that power had gone out from him. He turned around in the crowd and asked, "Who touched my clothes?"

"You see the people crowding against you," his disciples answered, "and yet you can ask, 'Who touched me?' "

But Jesus kept looking around to see who had done it. Then the woman, knowing what had happened to her, came and fell at his feet and, trembling with fear, told him the whole truth. He said to her, "Daughter, your faith has healed you. Go in peace and be freed from your suffering."

While Jesus was still speaking, some people came from the house of Jairus, the synagogue leader. "Your daughter is dead," they said. "Why bother the teacher anymore?"

Overhearing what they said, Jesus told him, "Don't be afraid; just believe."

He did not let anyone follow him except Peter, James and John the brother of James. When they came to the home of the synagogue leader, Jesus saw a commotion, with people crying

(cont'd next page)

and wailing loudly. He went in and said to them, "Why all this commotion and wailing? The child is not dead but asleep." But they laughed at him.

After he put them all out, he took the child's father and mother and the disciples who were with him, and went in where the child was. He took her by the hand and said to her, "*Talitha koum!*" (which means "Little girl, I say to you, get up!"). Immediately the girl stood up and began to walk around (she was twelve years old). At this they were completely astonished.

MARK 5:21-42

—CHAPTER 12—
The After Party!

A PHILANTHROPIST, an atheist, a father, and his young son were out for a Sunday afternoon flight on a small, private airplane. Upon reaching its desired altitude, the plane suddenly developed engine trouble. Despite the pilot's best efforts, the plane started to go down.

Frantically, the pilot rushed to the back of the plane and grabbed a parachute. He flung open the side hatch, yelled, "It's every man for himself," and jumped.

Shockingly, there were only three parachutes left. The philanthropist quickly snatched the first parachute and screamed, "I make the world a better place! I must live for the sake of humanity!" Then he jumped.

The atheist yelled out, "I'm one of the smartest people in the world and the Universe's gift to this world." Without reservation, he also grabbed a parachute and jumped to save his life.

The father instantly looked at his little boy and said, "Son, I love you more than anything. Take this last parachute. Jump, and live for Jesus."

The little boy immediately handed the parachute back to his father and said, "No, Dad, you can have it. The smartest man in the world just jumped out with my backpack."

DON'T BE STUPID

Psalm 14:1 says, "The fool says in his heart there is no God." Too harsh? They're not my words. God spoke them. But let me paraphrase this nugget of truth for you anyway: if you don't believe in God, you're stupid.

There. Is that better? I tried to say this as lovingly as possible. So, what does it mean to be smart then?

Let's flip the words in Psalm 14:1 to read, the wise say in their heart, there *is* a God.

And who is even wiser than that? Jesus tells us in John 11:26, "Whoever lives and believes in me shall never die." Believe in God, and you get wisdom. Decide to believe in Jesus, and He'll give you life.

Mark gives us two separate stories, intertwined as one, that point to this reality. These stories differ in many ways; they involve different people from different backgrounds with different problems. But these stories are similar, though, in at least one way—they both involve people who are smart enough to believe in Jesus and the life He offers.

In the verses above, Mark continues to place the focus on the magnetism of Jesus, the Life of the Party. Throughout the gospels, Jesus is constantly on the move, and He moves with expediency. Mark often employs the word *immediately* to connote Jesus' urgency to seek and save the lost.

Additionally, he emphasizes Jesus' absolute authority over death and disease wherever He goes. Jesus moves with purpose and power. In this story, Mark highlights the transforming life that flows from Jesus by telling us two different, but closely related stories.

It's very interesting how these two stories go together. The first story (involving Jairus) begins, but is then suddenly interrupted by the second one. Mark wraps up this second story, then goes back to finish the first one. The first story begins and ends the verses, while the second is in the middle.

There's a big theological seminarian term for this. Are you ready for it? It's called "sandwiching." *I know, it's really not that deep. But I bet you're hungry now!*

Yes, this approach really is referred to as "sandwiching," and it occurs nearly ten times in Mark's Gospel. The purpose of this particular and metaphorical culinary staple is to highlight the spontaneous grace of God through Jesus Christ.

Here's some tasty truth: the life and love of Christ can come upon anyone, at any time, anywhere, unexpectedly!

Both stories point to the loving power of Jesus and the importance of faith. And this second story, in the middle, isn't just a side story. It's not an "oh, and by the way" kind of story or some rabbit trail Mark is heading down.

Now Mark doesn't have ADHD. But he wants us to remember that Jesus is always on the move. And when Jesus is on the move, get ready, prepare yourself, and hold on tight, because He might do something extraordinary before He arrives at his intended destination.

And in this case, He does.

The second story, the inside portion of the sandwich, is exciting and important, not only because it reminds us of the spontaneous grace of God in Christ, but also because it's the key to interpreting the story on the outside.

Let's begin in the middle, with this second story.

Like any situation in the gospels involving Jesus, He is always the main character; He's always the central figure. But in this second story, there's another important figure—a sick woman who is hemorrhaging. Mark says she's been bleeding for 12 years and her condition is getting worse; it's slowly destroying her body and depleting her soul of any hope.

She doesn't have any friends. Because of the nature of her sickness, the fact that she's bleeding all the time, she's considered ceremonially unclean, which means she isn't able to go to the temple, and she's shunned by society.

She's an outcast who has been discarded and disregarded by her community because of her condition.

But despite her social status and despite her condition, she's still trying hard, like any of us would, to fight this disease. She's been to the best doctors in town and has spent all of her money on the latest and greatest healing concoctions. But nothing has worked, and she's desperate! This woman has exhausted all of her resources but one: Here comes Jesus.

The Son of God is within her reach. He's walking her way. She's heard about Jesus, about who He is, what He has done, and what He can do. She has embraced the rumors of His power as fact and begins to believe Jesus can give her exactly what she wants, exactly what she needs—healing.

Without question, she has faith in Jesus. This faith moves her to action. She's a bit hesitant, though, and doesn't want to make a scene by calling out to Jesus.

Knowing what we know about this woman, maybe it's because she has conflicting thoughts swirling around her brain. Thoughts like:

- *Well, Jesus would never stop for me if I call out to Him. I mean, who am I? I'm nobody. And He's Jesus! He's busy, way too busy for me.*
- *He's got more important things to do, more important people to see; in fact, He's on His way to heal that rich man's daughter right now.*
- *But if I can just get to Jesus and touch Him, maybe that's all it would take—.*
- *But, where do I touch Him, and how? I can't touch His head, that would be disrespectful; I can't grab His hand, that's too obvious and inappropriate....*
- *I know! I can touch His cloak. I can push through the crowd and just kind of brush up against Him. Yeah, that might work.*

Whatever the case may be, first her mind makes a move toward Jesus, then her body follows. She takes a step of faith and makes her way through the energized and curious crowd standing between her and Jesus.

At first, she probably moves timidly, trying to stay under the radar, unnoticed. But the crowd, just like life, begins to push her to the back. She's determined, though; nothing is going to stop her now.

She's been waiting 12 years for this moment. This is her opportunity! The Son of God is within her reach!

She pushes through the crowd, finally gets to Jesus, reaches around one of His disciples, and touches Jesus' cloak.

All of a sudden, an unfathomable degree of power is unleashed upon her body. Immediately, the indescribable, supernatural, divine life of God suddenly courses through her arteries and travels through her veins at the speed of light. Instantaneously, the bleeding stops.

What was that? Jesus thinks and immediately turns around. He knows something's up, but in His humanity, it appears He doesn't know *exactly* what happened. Jesus speaks up over the noisy, and nosey, crowd, "Who touched my clothes?"

Trembling with fear at Jesus' power, the woman falls at his feet, admits she was the one who unleashed the life within him, and tells Jesus her story. What's his response?

"Woman, are you crazy? What are you doing? I'm not some genie in a bottle that you rub to make your wishes come true." No. Jesus doesn't say that.

"Lady, look around you; you're not the only one who needs healing. Pick a number, get in line, and wait for your turn just like everybody else. Better yet, just ask next time!" Nope. Jesus doesn't say that, either.

Patiently and peacefully, Jesus looks at this former despondent and desperate woman and says, "Daughter, your faith has healed you."

Did you catch that? Jesus says, "Your faith . . . ."

Faith is the catalyst in this story. Who did the healing? Well, Jesus. Duh. Of course, it was Jesus. He's the life of this party once again. He has absolute authority over every disease. And yet, Jesus tells this woman she's the one responsible for her healing. He said, "Your faith has healed you." She exercised her faith in Jesus, and He changed her life. Her body, once oozing with blood, was now oozing with life.

Although it is the second story in this passage, it is where the first miracle occurs. Can you fathom the woman's joy? She, who was once ostracized, would undoubtedly become the most popular kid on the block.

What would you do if you were in her sandals? Throw a party? I would! And I'd invite the entire crowd, especially those who had disowned me for 12 years.

FACE-PLANTING IN THE PRESENCE OF JESUS

This new woman isn't the only one in this passage to exercise their faith, though. Remember? Mark tells us that Jairus employs his faith, too.

But unlike the bleeding woman, Jarius expresses his faith openly. Jairus doesn't approach Jesus under the cover of darkness like Nicodemus, nor incognito as the woman in this story does. Jairus falls at Jesus' feet. He falls flat on his face in the street, pleading with Jesus to cure his child.

This demonstrative act is a big deal and a bold move for Jairus. He's one of the leaders of the synagogue. He's prestigious, has a reputation to uphold with friends in high places, if you know what I mean—like the Pharisees and other members of the religious elite.

By the way, those Pharisees and the religious elite aren't exactly big fans of Jesus. Jairus' faith in Jesus isn't going to sit very well with them. They're not going to approve of his sudden pursuit of Jesus.

But Jairus doesn't care what they think; it doesn't matter to him if he has their approval to believe in Jesus or not.

Just like the bleeding woman, Jairus is desperate, as well. And he would rather lose his friends than lose his daughter.

So, when he catches wind that Jesus is within his reach, it's game on for him. Without giving it a second thought, he throws aside his pride, prestige, and even his dignity, runs to Jesus, falls down in the dirt at the feet of Jesus, and pleads for help.

Jesus immediately (*there's that word again*) agrees to help.

Hurriedly, the two of them, trailed by a crowd of spectators, made their way to Jairus' house. En route, Jairus' heart is instantly encouraged. Before he even arrives at his home, he witnesses a miracle.

A woman is healed by Jesus right before his very eyes. As Jairus is walking away from her healing, his faith in Jesus is likely at an all-time high. But it doesn't stay there long because shortly after, his faith is tested.

A few of his friends find Jairus and tell him that his sick daughter has died. "It's over, Jarius. Don't bother Jesus anymore. You're both too late."

I'm sure there were others in the crowd who began to whisper, "Well, I guess that's it. The show's over. Time for everyone to go home." Little did they know that it's never too late when *the Life of the Party* is on the move.

At this point, Jesus ignores all the naysayers and their little comments. Like always, Jesus doesn't respond to the ridiculous. Instead, He looks at Jairus. "Don't be afraid; just believe."

When they arrive, Jairus's home is loud and chaotic. Death is in the air, and it's dissonant. The whispers of hope once in the air, knowing that the healer was on His way, are quickly replaced with sounds of sorrow and despair. People are hysterically weeping and wailing. It's the customary thing to do. Some are even ancient-day paid professionals. But the crying turns to mockery when Jesus speaks.

He says, "The child is not dead but asleep," and these skeptics laugh at Him. It's pretty clear Jesus doesn't have any patience for these clowns. He has these jokers removed and invites the believers to accompany Him.

Jesus invites Jairus and his wife, Peter, James, and John with him to see this dead girl. With a heart full of compassion and love, Jesus kneels beside her. With the voice that calmed the storm, cast out demons, and created the universe, Jesus takes the hand of this precious 12-year-old girl and utters two words, "Talitha Koum." In Aramaic, it's translated, "Little girl, get up."

Once again, in a moment, the life of Christ is unleashed. The breath of God fills her lungs. Life kicks death in the jaw. More electric than all the defibrillators in the world combined, one divine spark reignites her heart.

She's alive. The same divine power that had left Jesus moments ago when the woman touched his cloak now comes upon this girl simply because Jesus spoke.

What a miracle!

And who performed this miracle? Jesus. Of course, it was Him, but, again, just like in the middle story, faith is also the catalyst of this story. This miracle really began when Jairus took those first steps of faith to Jesus.

So, there you go: story number one completed, miracle two proved. The sandwich has been made, and it's delicious.

Now let's take just a few moments to look at (or, better yet, eat) this biblical sandwich.

Initially, we can see that there's quite a contrast between these two stories stitched together, especially between the bleeding woman and Jairus. Jairus is a *somebody* in the eyes of society, and the woman is a *nobody*—we don't even know her name.

Jairus is prestigious and powerful and popular; the unnamed woman is insignificant to many and powerless and unknown.

Jairus is rich; the unnamed woman is poor. In fact, she's completely broke.

Jairus loudly, blatantly, and publicly proclaims his faith by falling at the feet of Jesus and pleading for help; the unnamed woman expresses her faith discreetly, quietly, and covertly.

There's definitely a contrast between these two people. There are many differences, but there are also many similarities.

Either one of them could have very easily tossed in the towel and thrown themselves a little pity party. Either of them could have decided it was a lot easier to wallow in their misery than to exercise their faith. Either of them could have come up with a million and one excuses why they shouldn't go to Jesus. Both Jairus and the woman could have decided to sit and do nothing. Still, neither one missed their opportunity to encounter Jesus.

They both were needy and desperate and had a problem they could not fix on their own. Both of them went to the only one who could fix their problem. Both of them found themselves at Jesus' feet because they both had faith in Jesus and took steps of faith toward Him. And because they both acted upon their faith, they experienced the supernatural power of God.

These two people went to Jesus, *the Life of the Party*, and they both went to Him by faith, because He was within both of their reaches.

And out of both of their stories comes this unbelievably joyful, indescribably profound reality...

Jesus is within your reach today. Jesus is always within your reach. You can go to Him at any time, and you don't need to have credentials to get to Him. You don't have to have an impressive resume, or social status, or even a shred of prestige. You don't need to go through a priest or phone a pastor. You don't need angels or saints to guide you to Him.

The Comforter has come. The Holy Spirit has arrived, and through the power and presence of the Holy Spirit, Jesus is always accessible. He's always present, always there, always available. He's also available to everyone: the rich and the poor, the strong and the weak, the sick and the well, the popular and the unpopular.

Your faith can be loud, bold, and strong (like Jairus), or it can be quiet, timid, and tame (like the unnamed woman).

It doesn't matter. What matters is that you "just believe," as Jesus said to Jairus, and take a step of faith toward Him.

Jesus stands ready and willing, and actually lovingly longing for each one of us to take steps of faith toward Him. In Matthew 11:28, Jesus says, "Come to me, all you who are weary and carrying heavy burdens, and I will give you rest."

Are you drowning in sorrow and despair? Jesus says, "Come to me!"

Do you feel desperate for hope and healing? The Great Physician says, "Come to me."

Maybe you're hungry for truth, searching for love, or longing for meaning, significance, and purpose. Christ says, "Come to me!"

Are you feeling dazed and confused, hopeless and lost, hurt and afraid, empty and dead inside? The Giver of Life says, "Come to me!"

For those who are overwhelmed by anxiety, lacking self-worth, feeling stressed out, and prone to worry, the Prince of Peace says, "Come to me!"

Anyone burdened by sin, guilt, and shame? The Savior says, "Come to me!"

Needing a miracle in your marriage, or wisdom at work, or happiness in your home? Jesus says, "Come to me!"

What a simple, but amazing invitation: "Come to me!"

But it's just that, an invitation. We have to do *something* in response to His invitation. We have to take Jesus up on His offer. We have to do our part.

We can't just sit on our hands and do nothing. And Jesus doesn't just want an RSVP. No, like Jarius and the unnamed woman in our story, He wants us to go to Him. That's what faith is. It isn't just belief; faith is belief in action; it's belief in motion, which means that faith takes effort.

If you want to unleash the power of God on your life, then—with all that is in you—go to Jesus. With every ounce of your being, push through the crowds and past the distractions of life. Lay down your pride, carve out some time each day to set down your phone, turn off the TV, log out of social media, and get to Jesus.

Fall at His feet and plead for help, or turn on some worship music and praise His name. Take a walk in the park and talk with Him, or kneel by your bedside and say a prayer of thanksgiving. Sit down on your family room sofa or on your living room chair by yourself, or with your family, and read God's word; soak in God's story of love.

Take steps of faith toward Jesus every day of your life. Reach out and touch the hand that is reaching out for yours. Jesus will touch you, and He will speak rest, life, and power into the depths of your soul. This is what He does. This is who He is.

He's *the Life of the Party*. He gives life in the here and now, and, at the same time, He offers an afterparty that's literally out of this world.

THOUGHT-PROVOKING PARTY FOOD

1. Faith is like a muscle; it needs to be exercised. Recall an experience in your life where your spiritual muscles grew, and you put your faith into motion.

2. Picture yourself, for over ten years, waking up expecting a change. The woman with the issue of blood waited nearly that long for her miracle,

even while under the care of numerous physicians. What traits must a Christian possess to show such unwavering faith?

3. Read John 11:26 again from your favorite version. What powerful, yet simple requirement does Jesus teach that will give us eternal life, even after death? What action(s) must be taken on our part?

4. What are the conflicting thoughts that often swirl around in your head when attempting to place your complete trust in Jesus? How do those thoughts contradict John 11:26?

—ABOUT THE AUTHOR—

JASON J. NELSON serves as one of the teaching pastors at Grace Woodlands Church and has accumulated over two decades of full-time ministry experience in both associate and senior pastoral roles. He is deeply committed to evangelism, discipleship, and leadership development, serving as the National Director of Expansion for the U.S. Pastor Council and Editor-in-Chief for The Forge Journal.

Before entering ministry full-time, Jason worked for seven years as an educator, administrator, and coach. His passion for public service also led him to serve two terms as an elected official on The Woodlands Township Board of Directors. He continues to influence public policy and governance through his involvement with several boards and committees that promote and impact governance with the values of the Kingdom.

Jason is the co-founder and President of Acts 17 Ministries, a non-profit organization devoted to making disciples and advancing the Gospel within political and governmental arenas around the world. He also serves as a professor of Bible and theology, training and mentoring the minds of current and future Christian leaders.

Jason holds B.A., M.A., M.Ed., M.Div., and Ph.D. degrees, as well as an honorary Doctorate of Divinity. He and his wife, Tiffany, have six children and live in The Woodlands, Texas.

www.ingramcontent.com/pod-product-compliance
Lightning Source LLC
Chambersburg PA
CBHW050643160426
43194CB00010B/1782